In the Absence of Fantasia

In the Absence of Fantasia

Troeltsch's Relation to Hegel

George J. Yamin, Jr.

University Press of Florida

GAINESVILLE □ TALLAHASSEE □ TAMPA □ BOCA RATON □ PENSACOLA □ ORLANDO □ MIAMI □ JACKSONVILLE

Copyright 1993 by the Board of Regents of the State of Florida

Printed in the United States of America on acid-free paper

The University Press of Florida is the scholarly publishing agency for the State University System of Florida, comprised of Florida A & M University, Florida Atlantic University, Florida International University, Florida State University, University of Central Florida, University of Florida, University of North Florida, University of South Florida, and University of West Florida.

Library of Congress Cataloging in Publication Data
Yamin, George J., 1955–
    In the absence of fantasia: Troeltsch's relation to Hegel/George J. Yamin, Jr.
      p. cm.
    Includes bibliographical references and index.
    ISBN 0-8130-1244-9
    1. Troeltsch, Ernst, 1865–1923.   2. Hegel, Georg Wilhelm Friedrich, 1770–1831—Influence.   3. History (Theology)—History of doctrines—19th century.   I. Title.
    BX4827.T7Y35   1993
    231.7′6′092—dc20   93-23758

Wallace Stevens, "The Course of a Particular," is from Stevens's *Opus Posthumous*, copyright 1957 by Elsie Stevens and Holly Stevens. Reprinted by permission of Alfred A. Knopf, Inc.

University Press of Florida
15 Northwest 15th Street
Gainesville, FL 32611

To my family

Today the leaves cry, hanging on branches swept by wind,
Yet the nothingness of winter becomes a little less.
It is still full of icy shades and shapen snow.

The leaves cry . . . One holds off and merely hears the cry.
It is a busy cry, concerning someone else.
And though one says that one is part of anything,

There is a conflict, there is a resistance involved;
And being part is an exertion that declines.
One feels the life of that which gives life as it is.

The leaves cry. It is not a cry of divine attention,
Nor the smoke-drift of puffed-out heroes, nor human cry.
It is the cry of leaves that do not transcend themselves.

In the absence of fantasia, without meaning more
Than they are in the final finding of the ear, in the thing
Itself, until, at last, the cry concerns no one at all.
                    —Wallace Stevens, "The Course of a Particular"

Contents

Acknowledgments

This essay was conceived and written in what in many ways now seems to me like another lifetime. Nonetheless, sufficient memories of that previous incarnation linger to allow me gratefully to thank the many individuals whose help made the completion of this project possible.

To the University Press of Florida, to Dr. Jeanne Ruppert, and to Elizabeth Johns and Michael Senecal, who edited my manuscript, I owe the opportunity to have this essay published in the first place, and in a version better than the one I submitted.

To Jo Ann Joyce I am grateful for her generous and capable assistance in transforming my translations of original German passages into accurate and readable English prose, to the extent that this is possible when dealing with Hegel and Troeltsch.

To Sue and Bryan Albro and to Bob Deitch I am obligated for their many gestures of friendship over the years we have known each other.

To Professors H. Ganse Little, Jr., and Mark C. Taylor, my teachers at Williams College, I am indebted for serving as the initial instruments of that "cunning of reason" that has directed my study of religion and theology since my days as an undergraduate student. To note that the topic of this essay represents, in some fashion, an *Aufhebung* of their respective interests can only begin to acknowledge the enormous influence that they both have exerted on my intellectual growth.

I am also appreciative to Professors Landgon Gilkey and Paul Ricoeur of the University of Chicago Divinity School, who served as readers of the dissertation from which this project originally arose. To Professor Brian A. Gerrish, my thesis adviser, I am especially grateful. The subject of my dissertation was chosen as much for the opportunity to work under Professor Gerrish as it was for my intrinsic interest in the thinkers and issues involved. From its inception, I was hopeful that the supervision of a mentor known for his high professional standards was the best possible way to ensure that the quality of my own work would be elevated to the highest possible level. In this regard, I was in no way disappointed.

Finally, I would like to express my deepest gratitude to my family, to whom this book is dedicated: my late grandfather, Arthur J. Watson; my in-laws, the family of George and Elizabeth Zimmerman; my sister, Mary, and my brother, Dave, who both continually use their own special gifts to raise and sustain my spirit; my wife, Margaret, who has shared in this and other academic ventures and with whom the best is yet to be; and my parents, George and Edna Yamin, who know no other way to foster the endeavors of their children than with unconditional support, unwavering faith, and relentless encouragement.

Abbreviations

AC   Ernst Troeltsch, *The Absoluteness of Christianity and the History of Religions*

GS   Troeltsch, *Gesammelte Schriften*

LPH   G. W. F. Hegel, *Lectures on the Philosophy of World History*

LPR   Hegel, *Lectures on the Philosophy of Religion*

PH   Hegel, *The Philosophy of History*

RSR   Troeltsch, "Religion and the Science of Religion"

SR   Troeltsch, "Die Selbständigkeit der Religion"

In the Absence of Fantasia

Troeltsch, Hegel, and the Changing Fiction

In *The Sense of an Ending*—his exploration of the nature and function of various fictions in our lives—literary critic Frank Kermode states that "men, like poets, rush 'into the middest,' *in medias res,* when they are born; they also die *in mediis rebus,* and to make sense of their span they need fictive concords with origins and ends, such as give meaning to lives and to poems."[1] According to Kermode, the most characteristic feature of our situation is its finitude; our historicity forever destines us to live out our lives entirely within time. We are caught inescapably between history's "ever-receding" beginning and its "ever-outstanding" end, which we can never join together.[2] Born well after history's opening tick, and dead long before its final tock, we find ourselves entrapped by a beginning we cannot remember and an end we can only anticipate.

Nonetheless, while an individual lifetime can never be coterminous with the span of world history, we still have a basic—even a primordial—need "to speak humanly of a life's importance in relation to [time]—a need in the moment of existence to belong, to be related to a beginning and to an end" (Kermode 4). In response to this fundamental urge, the human imagination generates fictions— models of world-time which render intelligible our abridged interval in the middle by fashioning "a universal plot, an enchanting order of beginning, middle, and end" (132). Fictions are created on various time scales. They range from the miniature versions which constitute the prose narratives of literature to the paradigmatic types— enduring fictions about reality as a whole which are "so persuasive that they [have] commanded general assent and [have] had the authority of truth."[3] At their most grandiose, fictions—by envisioning holistic structures within which beginning, middle, and end are coherently related—arrange the entire sweep of history. They thereby impose both overarching pattern and universal meaning on the temporal succession in the midst of which we live and die.[4]

Whatever their initial efficacy, however, the capacity of fictions to serve us has diminished noticeably with the passage of time. As times have changed, so too has our sense of historical reality. Fictions are themselves time-bound products. This quality has led to a varied appreciation of their validity and worth.

One of the most significant features of modern historical consciousness has been its recognition of our increasing remove from, and uncertainty about, ends and origins. In recent centuries, the insights and discoveries of the various natural sciences—especially biology, geology, and astronomy—have so extended our sense of the expanse of history that the beginnings of the human and natural world appear to be lost forever in the unfathomable depths of the past. Furthermore, there appears to be no necessary reason—barring some apocalyptic catastrophe of our own doing—for the extent of time that has yet to pass to be any less immense. The dubious status of cosmic beginnings and ends, in turn, has made us more sensitive to the two most characteristic features of temporal experience: the random successiveness of time's movement and the radical contingency of all individual historical moments. In the absence of any definitive beginning and predictable conclusion, history more and more becomes a process of indeterminate duration. Without these terminal coordinates to bestow form on the passage of time between them, we regard history's flow as disorganized flux lacking any meaningful sequential order, rather than as a narrative within which events unfold in a plotlike fashion toward an appointed end.[5] Our historical awareness has disclosed the apparently random linkage between temporal moments. Ongoing time has become nothing more than one damn thing after another. Moreover, amid the dynamic flow of history, events of the twentieth century provide compelling evidence for the brute contingency of all particular historical phenomena. These events include such unforeseeable and unexpected occurrences as the Holocaust, the detonation of nuclear weapons, and the atrocities and destruction associated with modern warfare, to name just the most horrific. Together they serve to prove, perhaps beyond reasonable doubt, that history is the realm not of the logically necessary or predictable, but of the radically new, different, improbable, and (unfortunately, in many cases) the overwhelmingly tragic, terrifying, and ghastly.

A consequence of such a perspective on history is an increasing scepticism concerning the explanatory power of the fictional paradigms. Under the pressure of reality, we have adopted an attitude of profound mistrust toward our inherited fictions. A respect for things as they are has led to a painful tension between historical fact and those fictions devised to structure the interval of lived time. In the face of our heightened temporal realism, once-successful fictional models, because of their seeming absurdity or irrelevance, have met their demise. Indeed, now "it may be harder than ever to accept the precedents of sense-making—to believe that any earlier way of satisfying one's need to know the shape of life in relation to the perspectives of time will suffice" (Kermode 3).

But intellectual doubt concerning the paradigms is accompanied by unassuaged emotional anxiety as we attempt to deal with our intractable historicity. Despite an increasingly critical stance toward them, our insurpassable desire for comfort or consolation demands that somehow we preserve or reconstruct paradigmatic fictions, rather than completely abolish or destroy them. Our finitude remains, as does our seemingly ineradicable urge to make sense of our experience. This finally guarantees that we will maintain an enduring relationship to these configurations. In the last analysis, our concurrent scepticism about the vitality of the paradigms and our unwillingness to relinquish them despite this suspicion reflect a genuine ambivalence toward all such creations, thus necessitating "a continuous preoccupation with the changing fiction" (Kermode 4).

Troeltsch and Hegel

In the last century, the German philosopher and theologian Ernst Troeltsch (1865–1923) was a prominent figure in the history of ideas who appreciated as much as any thinker the nature and significance of life lived amid the throes of time and change. His own intellectual career was shaped by an ongoing attempt responsibly to deal with the problem of historicism—the recognition that all things human emerge from and ultimately disappear into time.[6] Impelled by an ever-growing sensitivity to the weight of this problem, Troeltsch was repeatedly engaged in his writings with two related tasks: (1) a theoretical description of the nature of the temporal reality which serves as our setting, and (2) a deeply pragmatic evaluation of the implications of that description for religion, ethics, and culture.

In the course of his own efforts to make sense of the human condition, Troeltsch directly experienced the conflict between respect for the way things really are and our deep-seated need for existential comfort. He notified his readers of this fact in a lecture/essay written shortly before his death. In hindsight, Troeltsch acknowledged that at the root of his own intellectual life (and, indeed, the entire modern consciousness) was the fundamental antithesis between a critic's scepticism and the human tendency toward naive belief arising from our desire for consolation. Troeltsch's academic career was foreordained by two quite different and opposing factors—his broad-based education in the humanities and historical studies, and his religious and theological instruction. His secular training introduced him to the skills of rational criticism and the attitude of "clerkly scepticism"[7] appropriate to the historical task. These traits never left him and carried over to his pursuits in the many arenas in which he was active. "I was confronted, upon the one hand, with the perpetual flux of the historian's data, and the distrustful attitude of the historical critic towards conventional traditions, the real events of the past being, in his view, discoverable only as a reward of ceaseless toil, and then only with approximate accuracy."[8] But Troeltsch was also driven toward theology and philosophy—subjects which he "devoured with an equally passionate interest" (*Christian Thought* 6). These studies were inspired by "the interest in reaching a vital and effective religious position, which could alone furnish my life with a centre of reference for all practical questions, and could alone give meaning and purpose to reflection upon the things of this world. . . . I perceived the impulse in men towards a definite practical standpoint—the eagerness of the trusting soul to receive the divine revelation and to obey the divine commands" (5–6). From his two-pronged apprenticeship ultimately grew an awareness that the inner dynamism of his own thinking was propelled by a perennial conflict: the struggle between "the spirit of critical scepticism generated by the ceaseless flux and manifold contradictions within the sphere of history and the demand of the religious consciousness for certainty, for unity, and for peace" (8).

In his subsequent attempts to articulate and work through the problems posed by historical life, Troeltsch frequently turned to the past as a source for useful materials. In this regard, he was poised at an exceptionally fortuitous moment in time. His milieu was that of the major thinkers and movements which helped form the modern mind. In the theological realm, Troeltsch's position was defined and redefined in relation to the ideas of many of the leading figures of nineteenth-century liberal Christian thought, ranging from the early influence of his own teacher, Albrecht Ritschl, to that of the founder of modern theology, Friedrich Schleiermacher. In philosophical matters, he often flirted with the thought of Immanuel Kant and the so-called neo-Kantians of his own time. Additionally, Troeltsch was gradually drawn into debates initiated by the newly emergent scientific study of religion concerning the status of religion in the modern world. His own wide-ranging interests exposed him to the pioneering work of Max Weber and Karl Marx in the sociology of religion, William James in the psychology of religion, and the various members of the *religionsgeschichtliche Schule* who were applying the insights of the historical sciences to religious data. Troeltsch's own thought was thereby shaped by a legion of thinkers who must be counted among the major influences on modernity as it arose in the West. These thinkers served as his recurring debate partners as he analyzed and addressed the intimately related problems of history, religion, and culture.

Among post-Enlightenment figures, however, one prominent thinker—G. W. F. Hegel (1770–1831)—stands out as a pervasive and important part of Troeltsch's heritage. Troeltsch turned to Hegel as much as he did to any of his other predecessors as a primary resource in his examination and attempted resolution of this cluster of problems. In so doing, Troeltsch experienced very forcefully the impact of Hegel's profound philosophical reflection upon history. Hegel's posthumously published lecture series on this subject especially influenced Troeltsch as he grappled with the central problem of historicism and its many ramifications.

In the Western tradition, Hegel's philosophy of history stands as one of the greatest "sense-making paradigms, relative to time"

(Kermode 44). Hegel made sense of historical experience primarily by regarding history as nothing less than the story of the Absolute itself. According to Hegel, history is both the locus and the medium in which God proceeds from an initial stage of relative imperfection to a final stage of total perfection. At the outset of history, God exists in an incomplete state, lacking in self-knowledge. To overcome this deficiency, the divine objectifies itself in the world so that it can know itself in this externalized form. This process of self-recognition, however, is both gradual and cumulative. It occurs throughout the entirety of world history in a series of progressively more adequate approximations and is finally attained in the historical phenomenon of Christianity. For Hegel all of history is thereby the arena in which the ultimate identity (or dialectical unity) of God and world is revealed and the final self-realization of the Absolute is achieved.

Two significant implications for an interpretation of historical experience may be drawn from Hegel's philosophical vision of history. First, an intimate ontological relationship exists between the finite phenomena of history and the Infinite immanent within the entire historical process. Everything in the world is a manifestation of the divine life. Thus, from the perspective of the Absolute, the particular data of history (especially its nation-states) provide the necessary material within which the Absolute concretizes itself, and without which it would be unable to proceed towards its goal of self-perfection. From the point of view of the phenomena of history, a value transcending that of the merely relative or transitory is granted to them by virtue of this relationship to the Absolute. As incarnations of the divine, they are, in a sense, transformed, becoming something more than purely contingent realities.

Second, Hegel posited a dynamic interconnection among all the macrocosmic individuals of history, arranging its various nation-states in a sequence of evolutionary development determined by the dialectical self-movement of the Absolute. History was not a random process for Hegel. Rather, it consists of a series of stages and transitions of mutual significance. Each grows out of earlier ones and lays the foundation for those yet to occur. The flow of history is not chaotic but rather a uniform, progressive sequence directed toward a definite telos. Furthermore, according to Hegel, this telos of history is immanent in the historical process itself. In Hegel's estima-

tion, the complete self-realization of the divine and the final disclosure of the identity of God and world have already occurred in
Christianity, which thereby qualifies as the absolute religion. The
actual attainment of the final goal in turn confers a unity and rationale on the entire sequence. It gives to Hegel's vision of history the
sense of an ending requisite for a universalistic account of temporal
experience. Indeed, Hegel's philosophy of history is one of those
many "coherent patterns which, by the provision of an end, make
possible a satisfying consonance with the origins and with the
middle" (Kermode 17). Or, stated more simply, it "helps us to find
ends and beginnings" (11)—as all fictions do—from our location in
the midst of time.

Since its inception, the Hegelian paradigm of history has influenced enormously many subsequent thinkers who, like Hegel, have
ventured to make sense of historical life. Included are such diverse
figures as Karl Marx, Søren Kierkegaard, and, in our century, different representatives of the so-called analytic school of the philosophy of history.[9] In each case, Hegel's thought was subjected to
often violent criticism and vehement rejection. Yet, for all of this, it
still provided—in ways both confessed and unacknowledged—many
of the categories of reflection that these later thinkers employed in
their own sense-making endeavors. As part of the Hegelian lineage,
Ernst Troeltsch stands as the figure of greatest interest to this study.
In it, I offer a comprehensive and in-depth examination of
Troeltsch's relation to the thought of Hegel, as a means of exploring
how this particular legatee both criticized and appropriated the
Hegelian paradigm.

My central thesis in this essay is that Troeltsch's relation to Hegel
is best described as the "sceptical modification of a paradigmatic fiction" (Kermode 24). From his earliest writings to his final investigations into the philosophy of history, Troeltsch's reflection on Hegel's
thought is imbued with the spirit of clerkly scepticism. Seen in this
light, his career reflects the persistent effort to adjust the Hegelian
paradigm in the interest of reality. In response to his own seemingly
greater appreciation of real history, Troeltsch unflinchingly subjected the main features of Hegel's philosophical vision of history to
detailed and often devastating critical scrutiny.

Troeltsch's negative reading of Hegel is complicated. Troeltsch
argued that Hegel's understanding of history violated both the

inescapable contingency of historical objects (which for Troeltsch was one of their most essential features) and the real nature of historical becoming. First, Troeltsch argued that Hegel's claim concerning the identity of the finite and the Infinite in all historical objects was essentially self-defeating. Although Hegel intended by this assertion to affirm the inherent worth of the former, Troeltsch thought that he ultimately denied their real value by locating history's true significance at the level of the transhistorical Absolute and its progressive movement towards self-realization. Moreover, as part of his unyielding polemic against all monistic theories of historical life, Troeltsch opposed Hegel's view of history as a law-regulated process generated by the dialectical self-unfolding of the Absolute. For Troeltsch, any interpretation which construes historical existence as the by-product of an ontologically prior reality—either nature or the Idea—threatens the uniqueness and autonomy of all events and entities which constitute the historical world and must be discarded. Finally, Troeltsch rejected the Hegelian thesis that within history the Absolute manifested itself completely and finally in the Christian religion. Troeltsch's recognition of the temporal interrelatedness of all historical phenomena persuaded him that no absolute or radically different objects may ever appear in history. All such entities and occurrences are contingent upon their historical environment, and hence are individualized by a particular set of spatiotemporal circumstances.

Troeltsch also argued vigorously against Hegel's identification of historical change with the progressive movement of the divine Reason toward self-knowledge. By so doing, in Troeltsch's view, Hegel patterned historical development according to a superhistorical model. He thereby failed to recognize whatever design might be found in real history, when it is considered on its own terms. In addition, Troeltsch disputed any understanding of history which saw its movement as following a unilinear, evolutionary path. For Troeltsch, history is not without its continuities. Its flow, however, can never be reduced to a single narrative which proceeds in a unidirectional manner. On the contrary, history includes considerable flux and multiple developmental channels which must be discerned and acknowledged. Finally, Troeltsch objected to Hegel's view that the culmination of this allegedly progressive development was itself an immanent historical event. For Troeltsch, the claim by Hegel that the Absolute had reached its perfect form in Christianity, besides violating the individuality of all historical objects, repudiated the genuine open-endedness of history, whose futurity must be respected in any interpretation of historical "becoming" true to its real nature. Our inescapable location within time prohibits us from ever seeing the structure whole, a feat implicitly performed by Hegel.

Despite the sustained criticism of Hegel's thought found throughout his corpus, however, Troeltsch accepted, at least in modified form, certain key elements of the Hegelian paradigm. His own effort to make sense of history was often remarkably consonant with that of his predecessor, thereby demonstrating a subtle but unmistakable congruence with this antecedent fiction. Although he rejected Hegel's understanding of the movement of history in rigidly dialectical or evolutionary terms, Troeltsch nonetheless appropriated the general Hegelian principle of development in his own conceptualization of the flow of history. In so doing, Troeltsch sought to rescue historical becoming from being seen as thoroughly random or chaotic and to demonstrate some irreducible minimum of continuity amid history's seemingly endless meanderings. Moreover, while disavowing that actual history followed a dialectically necessary path, Troeltsch in his early and middle years discerned within the general history of the world (especially its religious history) some semblance of an orderly progression. In a manner reminiscent of the Hegelian scheme, this progression culminates in Christianity (although by the end of his life, Troeltsch was much less sanguine about asserting the supremacy of Christianity among the world religions in terms of any such developmental plan). Troeltsch also retained the basic teleological thrust of the Hegelian paradigm. However, he located the expected end of history outside of, rather than within, the historical process itself. By virtue of history's incompleteness, Troeltsch thereby denied that one may survey the entirety of history, as Hegel claimed to do. While Troeltsch assumed that it was possible in principle to expand one's interpretation of history to the level of universality, in practice he restricted himself to the theater of western European civilization. Finally, though sharply critical of Hegel's strict delineation of the relationship between the Absolute and ordinary history so central to his philosophy of history,

Troeltsch never renounced "the last and greatest fiction"—the "fiction of the Absolute."[10] For Troeltsch, as well as for Hegel, the divine Reason is ever-present within history. It thereby provides the metaphysical underpinning to, and ultimate validation of, all otherwise relative historical phenomena.

Troeltsch's reflection on history, then, entails both a crucial departure from the Hegelian paradigm and the maintenance of a real relation to that paradigm. In Troeltsch's thought, the internal dialogue between rational criticism and the need for the solace that paradigmatic fictions can provide eventuated in a "constantly changing, constantly more subtle" relationship with Hegel's philosophy of history (Kermode 24). The latter continued to undergird Troeltsch's way of making sense of human experience, subdued as it was by his scepticism and historical realism. Alternatively, Troeltsch's relation to Hegel illustrates one of complementarity with "discredited fictional systems" (61). Troeltsch's unyielding respect for historical reality precluded his uncritical or total appropriation of the Hegelian paradigm of history. By the same token, its inclusion within Troeltsch's own conceptual framework, though often in obscured form, demonstrates our "permanent need to live by the pattern rather than the fact, as indeed we must" (11).

In light of these observations, my main purpose is to outline Troeltsch's relation to Hegel throughout many of Troeltsch's most significant writings. In so doing, I will trace the relative degree of variance "from the paradigmatic base" (Kermode 35) which may be found there. In chapter 2 I discuss the Hegelian paradigm of history found in his *Vorlesungen über die Philosophie der Geschichte*, a discussion supplemented, where relevant, by reference to certain of his other writings.[11] For several reasons, it is both legitimate and prudent to restrict the analysis of Hegel essentially to one particular text. First, this was in fact the main work by Hegel which Troeltsch addressed in his efforts to come to terms with the Hegelian paradigm. Second, because of the systematic overall nature of Hegel's thought, such an important work incorporates many of the central concepts and themes which pervade his entire corpus, or at least points obliquely to issues raised and treated more thoroughly elsewhere.

Chapters 3–5 constitute the major analytical portion of this essay.

In these chapters, I look at Troeltsch as a critic of Hegel's fictional system. My exposition of Troeltsch's relationship to Hegel itself assumes somewhat of a developmental approach as I trace Troeltsch's nuanced critique of Hegel throughout his entire literary output. As it happens, Troeltsch's thinking on virtually any significant issue which he addressed was never static and unchanging. Rather, it often assumed many different forms throughout his career, undergoing frequent internal development not unlike the type of movement which he discerned, and to which he repeatedly pointed, in the historical process itself.[12] As a result, virtually any analysis of Troeltsch's views on a particular problem or thinker (including Hegel) demands that one consider how these views changed—as well as remained constant—over time.

A sensitivity to the wide chronological range of Troeltsch's writings, however, does not necessitate a comprehensive or exhaustive analysis of the Troeltschian corpus in order to do justice to the problem at hand. On the contrary, while respecting the span of Troeltsch's career, I have restricted my choice of relevant texts either to those which contain explicit commentary on Hegel or to those which are immediately pertinent to issues raised in texts that belong to the former category. Troeltsch's literary fund, of course, is much wider in scope than this procedure suggests.[13] Indeed, a partial explanation for his appeal as a man for all seasons in the intellectual world is the willing and proficient way in which he delved into the vast range of concerns relevant to the modern mind. I do refer, on occasion, to selections from Troeltsch's writings whose primary import lies in other channels of thought (for example, the social sciences, theology, ethics, and the history of ideas). In so doing, however, I hope not to obscure the main lines of my argument.

Unfortunately, perhaps, for my purposes, no major work by Troeltsch was ever directed in its entirety to Hegel (although, in fact, several of Troeltsch's most important texts contain sizeable and significant sections devoted to reasonably extended assessments of Hegel's thought). As a result, my examination of Troeltch's critique of Hegel must ultimately abstract this critique from his discussion of various interrelated issues, upon which he brought to bear his analysis of Hegel's views. For this reason, it is first necessary to establish from chapter to chapter the variable context within which

Troeltsch's commentary on Hegel is found. This is followed by a careful investigation of his critical relation to Hegel as the latter is set forth within this context.

My approach to this project, therefore, is itself very Troeltschian at heart. I combine a detailed historical review of Troeltsch's writings with a specific systematic perspective—namely, an analysis of Troeltsch's repeated efforts to come to terms with the Hegelian paradigm, so as to arrive at a more adequate understanding of life as it is lived within the parameters of history.[14] In chapter 3, I examine the influence of Hegel in selected writings of the early Troeltsch[15] that address the modern challenge to the survival of religion in general. In chapter 4, I consider Troeltsch's response to the crisis of religious values raised by the modern idea of history. I focus primarily on *Die Absolutheit des Christentums und die Religionsgeschichte* (1902), written by Troeltsch in the middle of his own career.[16] In chapter 5, I turn to Troeltsch's critique of Hegel as it is presented in *Der Historismus und seine Probleme.*[17] Written in the last years of his life, this imposing text provides the setting for his final and most severe assessment of the Hegelian paradigm.

Finally, in chapter 6, I present a summary-critique of Troeltsch's own constructive position, as this position may be gleaned from the discussion in the three preceding chapters of his relationship to Hegel. At this moment in history, Troeltsch himself stands to us as one of our own precedents of sense-making. His effort to make sense of life as lived in our temporal interlude, in light of his critical appropriation of the Hegelian paradigm, therefore deserves scrutiny from the perspective of our own spot of time. The contemporary preoccupation with the changing fiction requires that we take account of Troeltsch's endeavors, just as, in his own day, Troeltsch addressed Hegel's thought as one of his own antecedent fictions. Troeltsch himself, for whom the effort to relate historical knowledge to the present was an unending responsibility of the scholar, may be said implicitly to endorse this rationale. According to Troeltsch, the obverse side of the principle of analogy constitutive of the historical method is the fact that "the understanding of the present is always the final goal of all history. History is just the whole life experience of our race, which we have to remember as long and as well, to apply to our present existence as well and as closely, as we can. Every historical investigation works tacitly with these co-efficients; and it is avowedly the highest goal of history wherever history is conscious of itself as an organic science with a definite significance for the whole of our knowledge."[18]

As mediated by his critical response to Hegel, Troeltsch's attempt "to speak in terms of a modern reality . . . without forfeiting the use of the paradigm" (Kermode 106) generated a tension in his interpretation of history that demands the attention of anyone concerned with the nature and meaning of history. We now know a great deal about history, based upon the empirical events of our century and the appropriate inferences which we may draw from our awareness of the terrifying limitlessness of time. This knowledge provides us with a set of norms by which any interpretation of historical life must be judged. In light of these norms, Troeltsch's contribution to a modern understanding of historical reality which respects the irrefutable contingency, individuality, and flux of human experience in time certainly deserves acceptance. However, Troeltsch's assent to an Absolute which in some way transcends and secures the relative and successive data of history, and his retention of the category of development to describe historical becoming, are both rational bases to object to his project. The radically historicist position to which his analysis of historical experience inexorably drives him suggests that the validity of what emerges within time must be affirmed on its own terms. By appealing to a transhistorical ground to the phenomena of history, Troeltsch thus retreats deeply into the Hegelian paradigm. Additionally, in the face of his own heightened appreciation of the individuality characteristic of history, as well as the challenge to any narrative-like account of historical movement posed by our present sense of time's immeasurability, the usefulness of the concept of development endorsed by Troeltsch has grown increasingly problematic. "The process of sophisticating the paradigm" (27) is never-ending, and the recognition of the questionable value of the category of development, as well as of the fictive status of the Absolute, are logical and essential steps in this direction.

At the outset of *The Sense of an Ending*, Kermode suggests that "sense-making" may be undertaken at two different levels: poetry and criticism. "It is not expected of critics as it is of poets [and even philosophers] that they should help us to make sense of our lives; they are bound only to attempt the lesser feat of making sense of the ways we try to make sense of our lives" (3).[19] It is with an eye toward this second order of sense-making that my study of Troeltsch and Hegel is directed, and I hope it will enhance the collective enterprise of making sense of our lives in three ways. First, this study is, to the best of my knowledge, the first full-length exposition of Troeltsch's relation to Hegel.[20] Serious attention has indeed been given to Troeltsch's thought in general, to his philosophy of history, and to his relation to other significant figures in Western thought. The unique angle of vision of this study is designed to increase our appreciation of his achievement by showing how Troeltsch has drawn upon an important part of his intellectual heritage as the source for his own creative contribution to this tradition. By attempting to interpret Troeltsch from this perspective, many of the central features of his thought will more clearly be exposed, and the lasting value of his own inventive constructs pursuant to time will become more pronounced. Second, this study makes at least an indirect contribution to Hegel scholarship by adding to a growing number of essays which take notice of Hegel's philosophy of history.[21] It is, however, the first of which I am aware that demonstrates the way in which Hegel's understanding of history was both rejected and accepted by one of his most thoughtful and incisive interpreters. Thus, by attempting to make sense of how Troeltsch made sense of the Hegelian paradigm, the essential features of Hegel's philosophy of history stand out in bold relief. Its apparent weaknesses are made visible, as are at least the partial reasons for its resilience.

Finally, this study further illuminates a problem which has existential as well as intellectual import for all of us, beyond its relevance for the world of Troeltsch and Hegel scholarship. According to Alasdair MacIntyre, the reason for our persistent interest in many of the materials of our cultural tradition—even those which seem most dated or antiquated—is that the philosophical problems which they address "lie so close to permanent characteristics of human nature and human language."[22] If our interest in attempts at sense-making is truly grounded in a perpetual human need to understand the historical reality in the midst of which we find ourselves, then a warrant exists for continuing to explore and decipher these earlier efforts to gratify this insatiable desire. As the maim features of Troeltsch's relation to Hegel are identified and examined, the nature of our larger endeavor to understand life from our contemporary vantage point perhaps will be clarified as well. This will, I hope, reaffirm the notion that sense-making is indeed an "infallibly interesting" (Kermode 3) and, one may add, a particularly long-lasting topic of analysis.

The Hegelian Paradigm

Making sense of experience (especially its historical dimension) is a fundamental human enterprise. Awareness of our ineluctable historicity, coupled with the impulse to locate ourselves within the larger temporal framework in which we live and die, begets various attempts to envision the totality of history, from beginning to end. In this way we bestow meaning upon our historical environs.

In the history of Western ideas, one such attempt which may claim classic or paradigmatic status is the philosophy of history associated with G. W. F. Hegel. As one part of his monumental intellectual labors, Hegel offered a fundamentally philosophical interpretation of the historical process which is universal in its scope. Hegel endeavored to make sense of world history by seeing it as the self-unfolding of the ultimate principle of the cosmos, a principle which progressively realizes itself in time. "World history is the expression of the divine process which is a graduated progression in which the Spirit comes to know and realise itself and its own truth" (LPH 64). In his philosophy of history Hegel provides, in great depth and breadth, an account of this divine process constitutive of history. As an overture to my main task, I set forth in this chapter the Hegelian paradigm as it is found in his *Vorlesungen über die Philosophie der Geschichte.*

The Metaphysical Basis of History
The Task of the Philosophy of History
At the outset of the 1830 draft of his *Vorlesungen über die Philosophie der Geschichte,* Hegel defines the task he has undertaken

in these lectures. Anticipating the confusion and suspicion which his remarks may evoke in his audience, Hegel suggests that in contrast to ordinary history, his undertaking requires a word "of elucidation, or rather of justification." The philosophy of history, he says, is "nothing more than the application of *thought* to history." But, Hegel continues, such an endeavor, so conceived, is as problematic as it is inevitable. In Hegel's view we are thinking beings by nature and cannot avoid such activity, even if we should desire to do so. Yet, despite its inescapability, the philosophy of history has its dubious features. For Hegel, the thoughtful consideration of history implies an imposition of concepts of philosophy onto the objective data of history. This, in turn, subverts the proper relationship between thought and being (the data of reality) and may ultimately lead to a manipulation of the facts of history by philosophy, which "does not leave [history] as it is, but *forces it to conform* to its preconceived notions and *constructs a history a priori*" (LPH 25).

The questionable nature of the philosophy of history becomes even more transparent when it is compared to ordinary history.[1] In contrast to its philosophical counterpart, the main aim of this type of history is simply the attempt "to comprehend clearly what is and what has been, the events and deeds of the past" (LPH 26). Furthermore, the credibility of conventional historiography—unlike that of the philosophy of history—is ostensibly guaranteed by the willingness of historians to restrict themselves to the perception of the available data without the interference of their own conceptual apparatus. Ordinary history "gains in veracity the more strictly it confines itself to what is given" (LPH 26). Thus, traditional historical studies are predisposed to grant priority to the empirical facts of history over the independent concepts of the historian. This sets the methods of historiography seemingly at odds with the enterprise of the philosophy of history, creating the subtle impression that the former are superior to the latter for so doing.

Upon closer inspection, however, the alleged dichotomy between ordinary and philosophical history is not as great as it first appears. The activity of historiographers—like that of philosophers of history—contains a frequently overlooked conceptual dimension that is nonetheless present. "We can therefore lay it down as our first condition that history must be *apprehended accurately*. But general expressions such as *apprehend* and *accurately* are not without ambiguity. Even the ordinary, run-of-the-mill historian who believes and professes that his attitude is entirely receptive, that he is dedicated to the facts, is by no means passive in his thinking; he brings his categories with him, and they influence his vision of the data he has before him" (LPH 29).To substantiate this claim, Hegel itemizes the conceptual activity of practicing historians on three different levels. On the formal level, historians necessarily employ certain concepts (for example, the notion of causality) to identify links between events, or the reasons behind them, in their attempt to ascertain what happened in the past. Second, on the level of material practice, historiographers use certain preconceived ideas as actual explanatory principles for historical events, rather than see history as determined by arbitrary and random variables. To many historians, the events of history are better understood as the result of human motivation, such as the quest to establish justice in the world, rather than as the products of purely external or natural causes. Finally, Hegel accuses certain professional historians of introducing specific a priori fictions ("fabrications given out as facts" [LPH 135]) in their account of past history. These involve on the part of the historian conceptual intervention of the most fanciful sort, such as the bogus claims of some historians that there once existed a primeval people who were directly instructed by God.

In sum, Hegel's analysis of the activity of historians suggests that both historiography and the philosophy of history introduce a conceptual element, each in its own way, thus blurring the seemingly sharp distinction between them. In Hegel's view, neither historians nor philosophers of history can realistically claim to be distortion free in their scrutiny of historical data. Nevertheless, Hegel's critique of the philosophy of history is not totally unfounded. By his own admission, the philosophical consideration of history stands rightfully accused of importing into history at least one of its own ideas. The philosopher of history indeed presupposes an a priori element that is not assumed by the ordinary historian, a presupposition which thereby serves qualitatively to differentiate their respective enterprises. This a priori element is Reason or the Idea.[2] Hegel somewhat diffidently confesses that "admittedly, philosophy does follow an a priori method in so far as it presupposes the Idea. But the Idea is undoubtedly there, and reason is fully convinced of its presence" (LPH 30).

The Concept of Reason

According to Hegel, Reason is the central notion that philosophy introduces into its consideration of history, by means of which the latter is contemplated. "The main objection levelled at philosophy is that it imports its own thoughts into history and considers the latter in light of the former. But the only thought which philosophy brings with it is the simple idea of *reason*" (LPH 27). Almost all of his readers would surely agree, however, that the idea of Reason for Hegel is hardly simple. When understood as a cognitive activity of the knowing subject, reason is an essential epistemological category within the Hegelian philosophical system, and its special meaning (especially in contrast to the Kantian understanding) must be grasped. Here, however, Hegel does not designate a mode of cognition, but an objective reality which refers to the ultimate metaphysical principle of the universe—the equivalent, in philosophical terminology, of the theological concept of God.[3] In an early passage in his lectures, Hegel presents a rich, though concise, definition of this ultimate principle which unequivocally highlights its divine or metaphysical character. Reason "is *substance* and *infinite power;* it is itself the *infinite material* of all natural and spiritual life, the *infinite form* which activates this material content. It is *substance,* i.e., that through which and in which all reality has its being and subsistence; it is infinite *power,* for reason is sufficiently powerful to be able to create something more than just an ideal . . . and it is the infinite *content,* the essence and truth of everything, itself constituting the material on which it operates through its own activity" (LPH 27).

Hegel's vision of the ultimate principle of the cosmos, while highly complex, suggests analysis in terms of the dialectic of transcendence and immanence. His repetitive use of apophatic language—especially the qualifier *infinite*—indicates that in some elementary sense Hegel conceives of Reason as transcendent to the world. It is a reality wholly other to, or qualitatively different from, the natural and historical realms of finite things. Furthermore, by stating that Reason is both "infinite form" and "infinite power," Hegel identifies the creative potency of Reason as one of its distinguishing attributes. This attribute is also consistent with its status as a divinely transcendent reality. Yet Hegel also characterizes Reason as "infinite substance," "infinite material," and "infinite content." In so doing, he thereby affirms that Reason is in some way operative within, or even identical to, the world as its ontological ground or substratum. Reason, then, is not entirely or exclusively a transcendent reality, but is immanent within nature and history as well. By so defining Reason, Hegel's full doctrine of God thereby combines both the classical emphasis on God's transcendence found in the Western theological tradition and a view of the immanence of the divine principle within the world that is, to a somewhat lesser degree, also present in theistic notions in the West.[4]

Regardless of his nuanced definition of Reason, however, Hegel suggests how the task of the philosophy of history differs from that of more conventional historiographical methods. The trademark feature of philosophical history is its presupposition of the presence and reality of the divine Reason in the world, and its most fundamental responsibility is to discern and examine Reason's worldly activity, to attain "knowledge of the Idea in history" (LPH 12). Thus, unlike professional historians, who restrict themselves to ascertaining what has happened in the past, philosophers of history assume that there is something more—a metaphysical or divine depth—to natural and historical processes. Acting within the province of this special assumption, such philosophers must direct their efforts (as does Hegel in the remainder of his lectures) to identifying and clarifying the status and role of this ultimate reality in history, insofar as these may be apprehended by a human observer.

Reason's Relation to the World

After positing the reality of Reason as the fundamental presupposition of any philosophical interpretation of history, Hegel elucidates its relationship to the world-at-large. In addition to the brute assertion of Reason's presence in history, the philosophy of history affirms the thesis—repeated often in Hegel's lectures—that history is governed by Reason, or simply that Reason "has ruled and continues to rule in the world" (LPH 33). Hegel consistently and vigorously denied the view that the world (and, specifically, world history) is governed by chance or is in any way a random process. On the contrary, "we must bring to history the belief and conviction that the realm of the will is not at the mercy of contingency. That world history is governed by an ultimate design, that it is a rational process—whose rationality is not that of a particular subject, but a divine and absolute Reason—this is a proposition whose truth we must assume" (LPH 28). As Hegel notes, this appreciation of the fundamental rationality of the world is hardly unique to his own perspective on history. Rather, it represents an idea which has appeared intermittently for centuries within the Western philosophical and theological tradition but which, Hegel argues, only in his own philosophy of history has attained its most adequate conceptualization. Thus, in order to clarify his own understanding of the intelligibility of world history, Hegel briefly discusses two alternative views of the world which partially resemble, but also differ markedly from, that presented in his lectures: the view that reason permeates nature and the doctrine of divine providence.

The protoscientific view that reason is found in nature dates as far back as the ancient Greeks. This view envisioned the natural world as a law-regulated system whose phenomena can be explained by the existence and efficacy of certain controlling principles. The rationality of nature is a direct function of the presence and operation of universal and immutable laws (for example, gravity). These rules, in a sense, govern the events and processes of the natural sphere in a stable and predictable manner, and hence "are its inherent reason" (LPH 34).

Yet, while the Greek vision of reason in nature represented a major breakthrough in the history of thought, its insights were eventually superseded by the doctrine of divine providence traditionally identified with the Judeo-Christian heritage. This doctrine is the religious equivalent of the view that the world is a rational process, and not "a prey to chance and external, contingent causes" (LPH 35). Philosophers like Anaxagoras did not presuppose the active presence of a cosmic intelligence. Instead they relied on human observers to abstract the laws of nature from the available empirical data. In contrast, the doctrine of providence by definition assumes the existence of a divine legislator, who rules the world according to its own infinitely wise decree. From this perspective, the rationality of the world is not due to its intrinsic lawfulness but is a direct result of the activity of the divine will. Proponents of this doctrine affirm that the events of history, and especially the fate of all individuals, are directly governed and controlled by God. God is the benevolent power sustaining and guiding our destinies, in conformity with a particular (if often inscrutable) plan. In short, the doctrine of divine providence presupposes that "everything which happens in the world is determined by and commensurate with the divine government" (LPH 41) and so negates the view that chance and arbitrary forces dictate the course of human events.

But despite its apparent superiority over the naturalistic views of the Greeks, the doctrine of providence, in Hegel's view, is itself flawed and must in turn be translated into the terms of his own philosophical interpretation of reason in history.[5] First, according to Hegel, the classical doctrine of divine providence is rarely applied by believers on a sufficiently large scale, but is recognized only in isolated, individual cases. But such a limited view of the providential plan, from Hegel's perspective, hardly does justice to the power and wisdom of its divine executor, within whose range of control and influence the fate of "plants and insects," as well as "the destinies of entire nations and empires," falls (LPH 38).

Second, Christians often affirm that the providential plan is ultimately hidden from view and that we are presumptuous to try to comprehend it. Again, the traditional understanding of divine providence is defective in Hegel's opinion because it assumes that "the divine being is remote from all human things and transcends human knowledge" (LPH 37). Hegel rejects the agnostic view that it is impossible to know God in favor of the more satisfactory notion that God is by nature self-revelatory, and hence accessible to human knowledge. "If the name of God is to be more than an empty word, we must consider God as benevolent, or at least as in some way communicative" (LPH 38). For this reason, we are capable of knowing God, and, in fact, obligated to do so—provided, of course, we employ our rational faculties (rather than vague and subjective sentiments such as emotion, feeling, or intuition) as the proper mode of apprehending the divine reality.[6]

In addition to his explicit critique of the traditional doctrine of providence, Hegel criticizes this theological tenet for other reasons which remain tacit in these lectures. Despite their understatedness, however, they are crucial to understanding Hegel's conception that Reason governs the world. Hegel's response to the alleged inscrutability of the providential plan and his general doctrine of the divine Reason both suggest the inadequacy of the traditional notion of the divinity as a transcendent and unknowable agent acting outside of, and beyond, the historical process. Such a notion must be revised in light of a more viable understanding of God's nature. We must therefore come to terms with Hegel's notion of Reason as a self-positing entity in order to appreciate his understanding of Reason's sovereignty over history.

According to Hegel, the most essential feature of the divine principle of the cosmos is its actively self-expressive character. God "expresses himself and himself alone; he is that power whose nature is self-expression and whose expression can be perceived by reason" (LPH 67). In contrast to the independence and self-sufficiency characteristic of classical Western notions of God, Reason is compelled by its own inner logic to express or posit itself in (or as) an object beyond itself. It "brings itself into existence and carries itself into effect" (LPH 28). Not content to remain a self-enclosed entity, Reason produces out of the essence of its own being a secondary realm which we know as the finite world of nature and of history (especially the latter), but which is identical to Reason as its own externalized embodiment. "This, then, is how the Spirit acquires a content: it does not find its content outside itself, but makes itself its own object and its own content" (LPH 47). By virtue of this act, Reason manifests its creative powers (albeit along the lines of an untraditional, emanationist version of creation). More important, Reason in so doing exercises its divine governance over the world. It does so, however, not as a foreign sovereign, or an agent acting externally to the world (as in the case of the doctrine of divine providence). Rather, it prevails as a resident ruling power incumbent within the world—a world which, as a product of its own act of self-objectification, is nothing less than the "image and enactment of Reason itself" (LPH 28). By offering a dramatic reinterpretation of the nature of the deity (at least in relation to a more orthodox theism), Hegel can, within the framework of his own philosophical account of history, thereby offer an intelligible (yet distinctive) account of the longstanding view that Reason rules the world.

We may also approach Hegel's notion that the world is a rational process from a different angle. The rationality of history derives not merely from the fact that the world is under the sovereign guidance of the divine Reason as the latter's direct product. World history is also a rational process because it is directed toward a final goal or telos. "In history, we must look for a general design, the ultimate end of the world" (LPH 28). As it is approached and finally attained, this goal imparts an overall rationale to the entire course of history.

The underlying intentionality which moves history is the acquisition of self-knowledge or self-consciousness on the part of the divine Spirit. Its ultimate aim "is the attainment of knowledge; for the sole endeavour of Spirit is to know what it is in and for itself, and to reveal itself to itself in its true form. . . . This . . . is the universal goal of the Spirit and of history" (LPH 53).

But the final goal of the divine Spirit (and, thus, of world history) is not achieved immediately, at history's outset. Although the world as its own exfoliation is in truth another version of itself, Reason, at least at first glance, is unaware of this fact. Instead, it initially perceives the objective world of nature and history as alien to, or different from, itself. Nonetheless, despite this seeming duality between God and world, Reason strives over the multiphased course of history gradually to recognize or contemplate itself in the objective world which it has itself produced.[7] When the World Spirit finally attains knowledge of its fundamental identity with the world of finite things, its original agendum is at last satisfied. Its consciousness or knowledge of the world as other than itself is transformed into self-consciousness, and the ultimate goal of world history is concurrently reached.[8]

In sum, the foregoing analysis of the nature of Reason and its relationship to the world has highlighted the fundamental principles of Hegel's metaphysics of history, as well as the way in which Hegel's distinctive philosophical vision of history qualifies as a fiction. Hegel in these lectures attempts to make sense of world history in terms of the activity of the World Spirit. The World Spirit posits itself as the natural and historical world (history's grand beginning or opening tick) but does so only as a means of ultimately obtaining its own higher goal of self-knowledge (history's ultimate end or closing tock). The totality of world history has meaning for Hegel insofar as it is the essential process whereby the absolute principle of the cosmos objectifies itself in order to attain its own goals. "World history is the expression of the divine and absolute process of the Spirit in its highest forms, of the progression whereby it discovers its true nature and becomes conscious of itself" (LPH 65). To appreciate Hegel's philosophy of history at this point, however, is only to discern the Hegelian paradigm at its most basic level. We must now examine the precise relationship between the divine Reason and the phenomena "of history proper" (LPH 68) (the human agents and

national states of history). We must also consider Hegel's understanding of the dynamic flow of history as it progresses toward its
grand finale.

The Formal Logic of History

After affirming the metaphysical basis of world history, Hegel in the
remainder of the first volume of his *Vorlesungen über die Philosophie
der Geshichte* elucidates the formal logic of history.[9] Before analyz-
ing the actual content of history, Hegel presents the basic theoretical underpinnings of his overall philosophical interpretation of history. These tenets proceed from his fundamental assumption that
the historical process embodies in temporal form the divine principle of the cosmos.

The Synchronic Axis of History

THE MEANS USED BY REASON

Hegel's philosophical analysis of world history is informed by the
fundamental hypothesis that Reason rules the world. However,
despite its omnipotence (or, perhaps, precisely because of it),
Reason does not deign to exercise its sovereignty over history directly. On the contrary, the divine principle attains its ultimate goal of
self-realization by using certain finite phenomena of the world
"which confronts us directly in history" (LPH 68) as the indirect
means by which to accomplish its purposes. More specifically, the
wide array of deeds and actions performed by individual agents in
the course of world history serves as "the sum total of *instruments*
and means which the World Spirit employs" to satisfy its own needs
(LPH 74).

　　Hegel clarifies how the Spirit so implements its own goals by way
of a phenomenological analysis of human action. He argues that the
most prominent activity in history is motivated at its most elemental level by selfish intentions, private interest, or, to use the singular
term most associated with Hegel, human passions. "An initial *survey
of history* . . . would indicate that the actions of men are governed by
their needs, passions, and interests, by the attitudes and aims to
which these give rise, and by their own character and abilities; we
gain the impression that, in this scene of activity, these needs, pas-

sions, interests, etc., are the sole *motive forces*" (LPH 68).

As Hegel recognizes, his analysis of human action in the world is distasteful to many observers of humanity, who prefer to understand our behavior as driven by more lofty and noble intentions, such as patriotism, virtue, or morality. Despite the pejorative connotations of such terms as *passion*, however, Hegel adamantly insists that without the stimulus provided by purely personal or selfish interest, individuals have neither the willingness nor the ability to translate their desires into acts.

> If I put something into practice and give it a real existence, I must have some personal interest in doing so; I must be personally involved in it, and hope to obtain satisfaction through its accomplishment—in other words, my own interest must be at stake. To have an interest in something means to be implicated and involved in it, and an end which I am actively to pursue must in some way or other be my own end. It is my end which must be satisfied, even if the end for which I am working has many other sides to it which have nothing to do with me. [LPH 70]

Despite the prerequisite of a personal vested interest in their outcome, actions motivated by passion are not necessarily amoral. Although intuition suggests that such actions are opposed to all ethical or spiritual values, Hegel argues that the passions are, in effect, ethically neutral. As we seek our personal advantage, our motives may often be shared by others, so that a coincidence of private satisfaction, and the promotion of the greater good of the community to which we belong, may occur. Whatever fruits they may bear, however, to Hegel self-centered, passionate interest underlies all human action at its deepest roots, and to ignore or deny this fact is fundamentally to misunderstand human nature. Moreover, to assert that all activity is motivated by passion is actually to affirm something positive (rather than censorious) about our nature. For Hegel, the energizing force of passion is an absolute requirement for all significant accomplishments in the human realm. The degree to which we devote ourselves with single-minded dedication to attaining our goals, without wavering among various alternatives or dissipating our energy in other pursuits, directly determines the degree to which we will succeed. For this reason, passion provides the necessary ingredient in our efforts to accomplish goals which might otherwise be beyond our reach. It thus is a desirable feature of human behavior rather than one to be despised or scorned. "We may therefore conclude that nothing whatsoever has been accomplished without the active interest of those concerned in it; and since interest can be described as passion (in so far as the whole individuality, to the exclusion of all other actual or possible interests and aims, applies itself to an object with every fibre of the will, and concentrates all its needs and resources on attaining its end), we may say without qualification that *nothing great* has been accomplished in the world *without passion*" (LPH 73).

After positing passion's central place in the human realm, Hegel examines its role in the cosmic sphere. For Hegel, the divine Reason and human activity in world history are intimately related—a relation which he portrays metaphorically by describing history as the loom of a weaver and the divine Idea and human passions as the cross-stitching on this loom. The Idea and human passion "are the warp and weft in the fabric of world history. The Idea as such is the reality, and the passions are the arm which serve it" (LPH 71). Furthermore, Hegel explains precisely how human activity in the historical sphere may serve the larger purposes of the divine principle of the cosmos. According to Hegel, all actions have implications and consequences which transcend our intentions and even our conscious awareness, but which are nonetheless brought into existence by the deeds which we perform. Although we may seem to be acting solely to promote our own interests, our actions are often efficacious on more than one level. Such conduct may simultaneously fulfill both our own private ends and a higher goal of which we are largely ignorant but which is nevertheless carried out.

In order to explain the relationship between our immediate, conscious intentions and those which exceed our own expectations, Hegel appeals to the analogy of a person, motivated by revenge, who sets fire to another's house. However, in addition to gaining revenge by the successful act of arson (the deliberate goal), a sequence of secondary results is also set into motion "which have nothing to do with the original deed regarded purely in isolation" (LPH 75). In addition to the destruction of the victim's home, these results may include the incineration of adjacent property, due to the spreading of the conflagration, which, in turn, may lead to the loss of innocent life. Moreover, even beyond these ramifications, the arsonist may be arrested and convicted of criminal charges as a result of the original act (which is certainly not part of the initial intentions). Thus, what began as an act of revenge eventually recoils against the agent, leading to highly undesirable aftereffects. Hegel's analogy thus suggests that in order to appreciate the full and complete results of our activity, we must look beyond merely the conscious plans of the human agent. These results often include a host of consequences which extend far beyond our original intent.

Hegel illustrates this thesis by an actual historical example which specifies how human activity may initiate a chain of events unintended by the agent and so fulfill both the aims of Spirit and the agent's more private concerns. According to Hegel, the conduct of Julius Caesar in opposing his rivals, which left him as the sole ruler of the state, may be interpreted on one level as nothing more than the necessary response of an individual seeking his own private end of political self-preservation. Nevertheless, Caesar behaved in such a way that the net result of this power struggle among a small group was to transform the entire governmental structure of the Roman Empire from a republic ruled by a senatorial aristocracy to an empire governed by a single person. This transformation, in turn, produced effects that reverberated throughout the course of Western civilization. Thus, Hegel argues that in addition to furthering his own personal advantage, Caesar's deeds served the transindividual needs of the World Spirit. By stimulating the continued movement of world history along its larger course, the actions of such an individual allowed a new phase of world history, and hence, a new phase in the Spirit's movement toward greater self-knowledge, to emerge.

The activity of an individual like Caesar, however, is representative of the impact and effects which numerous great figures have had throughout history. Driven by their own personal needs and ambitions, such heroes of history—its politicians, generals, and sovereigns—provide almost irresistible leadership to the nations and peoples under their charge and so generate by their own decisive actions the events and deeds which constitute history's great moments. By envisioning, or at least intuiting, possibilities for humanity not foreseeable by the great majority, and by seeking to realize these possibilities by means of passionate, dedicated action, such individuals initiate the often-tumultuous events which bring about significant change in the course of history. These individuals "do not find their aims and vocation in the calm and regular system of the present, in the hallowed order of things as they are. Indeed, their justification does not lie in the prevailing situation, for they draw their inspiration from another source, from that hidden spirit whose hour is near but which still lies beneath the surface and seeks to break out without yet having attained an existence in the present. . . . Such individuals know what is necessary and timely, and have an inner vision of what it is" (LPH 83).

It is unfortunate for the individuals in question, however, that once they have furthered the ends of the World Spirit, these great personages appear inevitably to meet an unkind fate. While they may have had the good fortune to have been the primary facilitators of the divine plan, this benefit is mitigated by their seemingly universal failure to obtain lasting personal satisfaction or happiness. Witness, for example, the early death of Alexander the Great, the assassination of Julius Caesar, and the exile of Napoleon. Indeed, in Hegel's view, the attainment of happiness by any individual in history, and especially its great ones, is an extremely rare occurrence. "History is not the soil in which happiness grows. The periods of happiness in it are the blank pages of history" (LPH 79). Such, however, is the method and genius of the divine Spirit, which reaps all the benefits of human activity, while the costs are absorbed entirely by the agents involved. According to Hegel, the divine Reason necessarily employs history's various agents as the instruments of its own purposes, while at the same time staying above the fray or behind the scenes of world history. It thereby remains unmolested by the exigencies and vagaries of history. Such, indeed, is the cunning of Reason.

> The particular interests of passion cannot . . . be separated from the realisation of the universal; for the universal arises out of the particular and determinate and its negation. The particular has its own interests in world history; it is of a finite nature, and as such, it must perish. Particular interests contend with one another, and some are destroyed in the process. But it is from this very conflict and destruction of particular things that the universal emerges, and it remains

unscathed itself. For it is not the universal Idea which enters into opposition, conflict, and danger; it keeps itself in the background, untouched and unharmed, and sends forth the particular interests of passion to fight and wear themselves out in its stead. It is what we may call the *cunning of reason* that it sets the passions to work in its service, so that the agents by which it gives itself existence must pay the penalty and suffer the loss. . . . The particular is as a rule inadequate in relation to the universal, and individuals are sacrificed and abandoned as a result. The Idea pays the tribute which existence and the transient world exact, but it pays it through the passions of individuals rather than out of its own resources. [LPH 89][10]

THE MATERIAL USED BY REASON

One of the most interesting features of Hegel's vision of the historical process is that it is curiously binocular. Hegel can cast one eye on the individual agents of history, envisioning their function and relevance in the course of world history as the primary means that the World Spirit uses to attain its goals. Yet Hegel's purview of historical phenomena is not totally microscopic. On the contrary, he is equally able to scan history in a more telescopic manner. Included in this panorama are the more enduring suprapersonal entities of the historical world—its societies, its cultures, even its civilizations. Alternatively, Hegel's attempt to make sense of history in philosophical terms measures the phenomena of history according to two different time scales. Hegel deals philosophically both with the short term of an individual lifespan and with the long term of the objects of history mentioned above. Nevertheless, whether one speaks of a shift in focus or a change in scale, Hegel can state that history's true individuals are those collectivities perceivable when one sees the big picture. "In world history . . . the individuals we are concerned with are nations, totalities, states" (LPH 36), while history's individual actors, when seen from a distance, tend to fade into insignificance.

If we may characterize Reason's relationship to the human individuals of history as utilitarian, we may define its relationship to the various nation-states of world history as ontological. The World Spirit employs human agents as the primary ways and means by which it attains its ends in history. The function and value of these individuals are therefore assessed in terms of their practical utility. Hegel sees the relationship between the World Spirit and the various nation-states of history, however, quite differently. History's individual actors serve Reason as the means to reaching its goals. The nation-states of history provide the divine principle with the primary material through which it may manifest itself in history, with "the form it assumes in reality" (LPH 93).

The most basic presupposition of Hegel's philosophy of history is that the World Spirit is immanent within the entire historical process as its underlying ontological ground. More precisely, however, Reason manifests or incarnates itself within the various nation-states of history. Reason "assumes varying shapes; but in none of them is it more obviously an end than in that whereby the Spirit explicates and manifests itself in the endlessly varying forms which we call nations" (LPH 28). For this reason, Hegel postulates that Reason indeed has an intimate relationship—a sharing of ontological substance—with the national individuals of world history. These individuals represent the actual external media which Reason assumes by virtue of its self-positing in the historical world.

In his examination of the status of the nation-state in world history, Hegel unfortunately does not define concisely how he understands this term. We may infer such a definition, however, based on Hegel's observations regarding what a nation-state is not. According to Hegel, the concept of a nation-state is not exhausted by its political connotations. It refers instead to a many-sided reality which includes and integrates within itself all the features of existence which are constitutive of human life-in-community. Within Hegel's understanding of national life, the political sphere is indeed a central component, and Hegel devotes his writings in political philosophy to a careful analysis of the basic forms of political government and administration which define and regulate the relationship between ruler and ruled that have emerged in the course of world history.[11] Nevertheless, the nation-state in history encompasses more than its constitution. Rather, it is an organic whole made up of multiple parts, all of which are intimately interrelated. Simply stated, a state may be defined as a constellation or configuration of particular historical events, social institutions, and cultural phenomena which share a certain spatiotemporal matrix, thereby conferring upon its citizens a sense of collective identity that sets them apart from other similar entities.

In the course of itemizing the various spheres which make up a nation-state, Hegel identifies a wide variety of components which constitute, to a greater or lesser degree of importance, the totality of national life. In addition to a nation's constitutional system, these include its system of justice and laws, the various forms of industry and trade which make up its economic activity, its artistic achievements, its diverse learned disciplines or modes of secular knowledge (ranging from philosophy to the natural sciences), its various codes of ethics and custom, and the armed forces and diplomatic agencies which regulate its international relations during times both of war and peace. In Hegel's view, however, the dimension of national existence which possesses pride of place is its religion, especially its concept or idea of God. But to what does religion owe its privileged standing within the organism that is the nation? Hegel defines the religious consciousness at its essence as the consciousness or awareness of God or the Absolute Spirit. Insofar, however, as God is, by definition, equatable with, or identical to, eternal truth, the religion of a nation provides its members with the most direct mode of access to, or knowledge of, what is universally true. It "is the consciousness of truth in its purest and most undivided determination" (LPH 105). By virtue of its acquaintance with the truth, then, a nation's religion provides its people with the standard by which all other activities or modes of knowledge can take their measure. "Everything else which can be defined as true is the concern of all men in so far as it has a corresponding principle within religion. To this extent, religion . . . constitutes the universal horizon and foundation of a nation's existence. It is in terms of religion that a nation defines what it considers to be true" (LPH 105).

The relation which religion has with other forms of national life varies considerably, depending upon the degree to which these other forms are themselves concerned with knowledge of the truth. Such dimensions of national life as a state's economic system or modes of warfare will have only a tangential relationship to religion. In contrast, the aesthetic and philosophical activity of a culture both share a profound interest in questions of truth-claims (albeit in fundamentally different ways), and so both will be intimately bound up with the state of religious knowledge which a nation possesses.[12]

Nevertheless, despite the relative differences among the other branches of national life in their relationship to a nation's religion, its preeminent status as the "common denominator" (LPH 111) of all particular areas of a culture or civilization is without challenge. For this reason, the variable degree of religious awareness on the part of different nations provides the proper focus for my later discussion of Hegel's actual philosophical analysis of these entities which constitutes his material philosophy of history.

The Diachronic Axis of History

Despite the fundamental differences which exist between the individual agents of history and its particular nation-states, in Hegel's analysis of the synchronic phenomena of history these entities share a significant characteristic which links them together in important ways. This common trait is their mortality. Hegel understood these two different classes of historical individuals to have a qualitatively different status and function in his philosophical interpretation of world history. In the final analysis, however, all individuals of history are perishable entities ultimately doomed to oblivion. Whatever may be their historical significance, "both [human] individuals and nations die a natural death" (LPH 59). Although the major civilizations and cultures of world history are relatively more enduring and long-lasting than other phenomena which arise in the course of history, Hegel insists that even these historical forms are subject to the ravages of time. Whatever heights of prominence and grandeur they may attain, their inevitable destiny is a gradual experience of decline and fall and an ultimate disappearance from the historical scene altogether. This fact is the source of considerable melancholy to the sensitive observer of history. "It oppresses us to think that the richest forms and the finest manifestations of life must perish in history, and that we walk amidst the ruins of excellence. History cuts us off from the finest and noblest of our interests; the passions have destroyed them, for they are transient. It seems that all must perish and that nothing endures" (LPH 32). In light of their ephemeral nature, the nation-states of history are a rather curious hybrid form. Coincidentally, they are both spiritual individuals (insofar as they are manifestations of the World Spirit in time) and yet also natural entities whose lifetime follows the basic pattern of birth, maturation, decay and degeneration, and finally death, endemic to all phenomena of nature. "The national spirit is a natural individual, and as such, it blossoms, grows strong, then fades away and dies" (LPH 58).

The recognition of the intrinsic mortality of all historical individuals provides the impetus to a consideration of history's dynamic quality. That all individuals in history are born to die stimulates the philosopher to confront the reality of historical change. History is a process of flux and transformation as much as it is the sum total of discrete, particular entities found in the past. "The first category [of historical analysis] comes from our observation of the changing individuals, nations, and states which flourish for a while, capture our interest, and then disappear. This is the category of *change*" (LPH 31). But for Hegel there is more to the reality of historical change than its negative aspect. An awareness of the fundamental transience of all things reflects only one side of the diachronic movement of history. The sadness that comes from a recognition that all must perish in history is alleviated by an awareness of the positive side of change: the reality of rejuvenation in history. The basic rhythm of history is such that the disappearance of one individual in time is inevitably followed by the emergence of new ones. In their turn the latter also pass away, giving way to yet other historical creations. "Out of death, new life arises" (LPH 32). For Hegel, history is equally the locus of the birth, as well as the demise, of the various individuals of history, and any effort to grasp the reality of historical change must come to terms with both dimensions of historical becoming.

His empirical observation of the dual-sidedness of historical change, however, is only a preliminary step in Hegel's efforts to discern pattern and meaning amid the flow of world history. The awareness of the rhythm of death and rebirth generated by the transience of historical entities and of the implicit rejuvenatory powers within the depths of historical life in turn raises the perplexing question of how to construe the "restless succession" (LPH 31) of individuals in history. Is history nothing more than "a motley confusion which draws us into its interests, and when one thing disappears, another at once takes its place" (LPH 32)? Or may we discern some semblance of continuity, as we observe one historical form give way to the next in the stream of history? Furthermore, if in fact we can identify a pattern of continuity in world history, what explanatory principle best accounts for the perpetual transition that constitutes the historical process?

In response to these basic questions, Hegel examines two alternative explanations of the pattern of world history. The first theoretical model is drawn from the world of nature. The various forms of life which emerge in the natural world are essentially no different than the antecedent life-forms which produce them or the subsequent life-forms to which they themselves give rise. For this reason, change in nature is fundamentally cyclical. Each generation of any given species reenacts the basic template of existence of its parent generation, one which it transmits in turn to its own offspring. "The reawakening of nature is merely the repetition of one and the same process; it is a tedious chronicle in which the same cycle recurs again and again. There is nothing new under the sun" (LPH 61). For Hegel, however, the notion of cyclical or perennial change inadequately describes historical change, and he rejects it in favor of a different model. According to Hegel, the transition in history from one entity to another is better understood in terms not of circular movement but of a developmental process in which each historical life-form represents a higher form than its predecessor. In this scheme of things, historical transition represents a movement of progressive, not repetitive, change. Under "the sun of the Spirit," movement and progression "do not repeat themselves, for the changing aspect of the Spirit as it passes through endlessly varying forms is essentially progress" (LPH 61). "Historical change in the abstract sense has long been interpreted in general terms as embodying some kind of progress towards a better and more perfect condition. Changes in the natural world, no matter how great their variety, exhibit only an eternally recurring cycle; for in nature there is nothing new under the sun, and in this respect its manifold play of forms produces an effect of boredom. Only in those changes which take place in the spiritual sphere does anything new emerge" (LPH 124–25).

According to the developmental or evolutionary model of historical change which Hegel proposes, however, the emergence of new historical forms does not entail the total obliteration of those less-advanced forms which have preceded them. Historical change involves not only the movement beyond past forms (which constitutes the moment of progress in history). The newly emergent historical object also retains a semblance of continuity with its predecessor by preserving within itself the essential truth of this ante-cedent form. Hegel unites in dialectical tension these opposing viewpoints—history as a sequence of ever-new and different forms and as the perpetual recurrence of forms which are ever-the-same—by introducing the principle of *Aufhebung* as definitive of true his-torical change. Aufhebung is a technical term in Hegel's system which means simultaneously to supersede and to include. The move-ment of history neither abolishes all previous forms nor repeats them identically. Instead, it embodies a kind of progress-within-regression as the stream of history surges forward.

Hegel's understanding of historical change as a progressive move-ment inevitably raises the issue of the criterion by which to measure such progress. If history is indeed an evolutionary process of con-tinuous growth from a lower to a higher stage, then the nature of "the guiding principle of development" (LPH 127) must be clarified in order to make sense of the passage of history. Such a principle may be gleaned from Hegel's assertion that history's ultimate telos is the attainment of self-knowledge by the World Spirit immanent within the historical process. The course of world history, in Hegel's view, is not "a process of infinite duration" or "an indeterminate advance ad infinitum" (LPH 149). On the contrary, historical move-ment culminates when Spirit achieves the goal of self-realization toward which it has been striving throughout the entirety of history. Seen in the light of this final telos, each phase of history (or, more precisely, each historical nation-state) represents an increasingly more adequate stage in Spirit's quest for self-knowledge. World his-tory is the progressive ascent of the divine Spirit as it moves relent-lessly towards its goal of self-recognition. In the course of this move-ment, each nation-state represents a link in this chain of development. As one passes away from history, another, more satis-factory manifestation of the Absolute Spirit takes its place. The activity of the World Spirit, therefore,

> is that of knowing and recognising itself, but it accomplishes this in gradual stages rather than at a single step. Each new individual national spirit represents a new stage in the con-quering march of the World Spirit as it wins its way to con-sciousness and freedom. The death of a national spirit is a transition to new life, but not as in nature, where the death of

one individual gives life to another individual of the same kind. On the contrary, the World Spirit progresses from lower determinations to higher principles and concepts of its own nature, to more fully developed expressions of its Idea. [LPH 63]

Hegel's Material Philosophy of History

One of the most fundamental axioms of the Hegelian system is the distinction between what is concrete and what remains abstract. "I wish, from the outset, to emphasize this distinction between a definition, principle, or truth which remains abstract, and one whose specific determination and concrete development are also explained" (LPH 35). In Hegel's philosophy of history, the distinction between empty formalism and that which assumes a concrete, determinate shape becomes the difference between the fundamental philosophical principles which underlie world history as they may be identified in abstraction from the actual data of history, and the concrete material of the human past. The more formal features of Hegel's philosophy of history thus represent a necessary but insufficient moment in his overall interpretation of the history of the world. We must turn finally to Hegel's survey of world history, found in the second half of his *Vorlesungen über die Philosophie der Geschichte*, to appreciate how the basic presuppositions of the Hegelian paradigm are determinately applied to historical data.

Unfortunately for the commentator on Hegel's material philosophy of history, however, his lectures contain a wealth—even, at times, a morass—of empirical detail, so that wading into them is forbidding. For this reason, I will focus on Hegel's analysis of the historical development of the religious consciousness, as the most useful index to his account of world history in general. In this account, Hegel includes much more than the various religions which have emerged in history. However, we may justify exclusive concentration on religious history based on several factors intrinsic to Hegel's philosophical analysis of history. First, Hegel's reflection on the relationship between specialized and philosophical history, presented in the first draft of his lecture series, provides reasonable methodological grounds for this choice. As defined by Hegel, the task of the specialized historian is to write a history of the world by selecting a partial perspective (for example, the history of art, law, or religion) that illuminates the whole of national life. This enterprise is more or less valid, depending on whether the chosen branch of national activity is "directly related to the history of the nation as a whole" (LPH 23). Because religion, according to Hegel, is the cornerstone of all other features of nationhood, we may single out the religious dimension of civilization as its most essential feature. Second, Hegel's philosophy of history rests on the basic metaphysical or religious principle that world history consists of the self-unfolding of the divine Reason. Thus, insofar as the idea or concept of God prevalent at any given historical moment directly mirrors the stage of Spirit's self-expression, the religious aspects of life can serve as a reliable indicator of historical development at its most profound levels.[13] For these reasons, I analyze Hegel's material philosophy of history in terms of his account of the history of religious consciousness, thereby providing an abbreviated synopsis of Hegel's philosophy of the history of religion.[14]

Hegel's material philosophy of history relies on a periodization which subdivides history into three main phases: the Oriental world, the Greco-Roman world, and the Germanic-Christian world. Any survey of the development of world history must begin with the great civilizations of the Orient, proceed to the cradle of Western culture (the civilizations of Greece and Rome), and conclude with a consideration of Christendom as it is localized in Western Europe. "World history travels from east to west; for Europe is the absolute end of history, just as Asia is the beginning" (LPH 197). Hegel's tripartite division of world history in his *Vorlesungen über die Philosophie der Geschichte* roughly corresponds to his three-part classification of world religion in his *Lectures on the Philosophy of Religion*.[15] In the latter, Hegel identifies three main types of religion, which may be associated, respectively, with the Oriental, the Greco-Roman, and the Germanic-Christian worlds: immediate or natural religion, religion characterized by the elevation of the spiritual over the natural, and the consummate religion. The distinguishing features of each of these basic categories of religion (especially their notions of divinity) illustrate the nature of historical progress which Hegel discerns in the movement of world history from Orient to Occident. Each phase in the development of the religious consciousness contains an element of truth. Each as well has a particular failing which propels religious history forward until it reaches its culmination in historical Christianity. "Every form of spiritual force, and *a fortiori* every religion is of such a nature, that whatever be its peculiar character, an affirmative element is necessarily contained in it. However erroneous a religion may be, it possesses truth, although in a mutilated phase. In every religion there is a divine presence, a divine relation; and a philosophy of history has to seek out the spiritual element even in the most imperfect forms" (PH 195–96).

The first major phase of world history which Hegel considers in his extensive survey of the human past is the Oriental world. Within the realm of the East, Hegel examines the world-historical civilizations associated with China, India, and Persia (and, to a lesser extent, Syria and Egypt), as well as the determinate religions which have manifested themselves there. These include, among others, the various religions of China; Hinduism and Buddhism (the religions of India); and Zoroastrianism. Although the various Eastern religions are not a completely homogeneous group, Hegel suggests that, for purposes of typification, they belong to nature religion. This form of the religious principle is characterized by a monistic worldview which fails to distinguish the spiritual realm from the realm of nature, stressing instead the oneness of all reality. Nature religion "is the unity of the spiritual and the natural, where the spirit still is in unity with nature" (LPR 207). "In the Oriental spirit there remains as a basis the massive substantiality of Spirit immersed in nature" (PH 220).

From this religious perspective, a specific notion of God (or ultimate reality) emerges. By virtue of the mutual coinherence of the spiritual and the natural, God is considered in highly impersonal terms. The divine is that absolute power and substance which pervades and underlies the whole of finite reality as its primordial ground and source and its principle of unity. An essentially pantheistic concept of God is thus the most distinctive trait of this most rudimentary form of the religious consciousness.

This idea of divine reality (at least in attenuated form) is present in all of the religions of the East. Hinduism, however, is the religion of nature par excellence. "The dreaming unity of Spirit and nature, which involves a monstrous bewilderment in regard to all phenomena and relations, we have already recognized as the principle of the

Hindu spirit" (PH 155). Its central concept of Brahman best exemplifies the notion of God characteristic of this early developmental stage of religion.[16] According to classical Indian thought, Brahman designates the sole reality which permeates the entirety of the cosmos. As "the substantial unity of All" (PH 148), it lies at the basis of all things. Considered in itself, Brahman stands for pure, undifferentiated being. It is beyond all limiting qualities. Hence, no attributes can be assigned to it. As the ultimate reality, however, Brahman is also the creative ground or intelligent cause of the world of human experience. Brahman is "substance in its simplicity, which by its very nature expands itself into the limitless variety of phenomenal diversities. For this abstraction, this pure unity, is that which lies at the foundation of all—the root of all definite existence" (PH 156).

Within the Hindu tradition, the world of multiplicity (which includes all individual selves) is the product of Brahman and emanates from the ultimate principle. As such, its multifarious entities may each claim to be incarnations or manifestations of the Absolute. These incarnations range from inanimate objects and animals to the innumerable avatars of Brahman worshipped by various cults within Hinduism. "The Indian view of things is a universal pantheism. . . . One substance pervades the whole of things, and all individualizations are directly vitalized and animated into particular powers. . . . Everything, therefore—sun, moon, stars, the Ganges, the Indus, beasts, flowers—everything is a God to it" (PH 141). Despite all appearances, however, this world of finite things is devoid of any real substantiality. Brought forth by a spontaneous release of creative energy on the part of Brahman, the world is finally reabsorbed in the ultimate reality. This cyclic pattern repeats itself endlessly over the eons.

From Hegel's point of view, the religious principle of the Oriental world contains a glimmer of truth about the nature of God as immanent within the world, and so identical to it. It is, however, unsatisfactory. This perspective regards the realm of finite being as never more than a temporary manifestation of the absolute substance. Its existence is only an illusion. The world of finitude "fall[s] outside that abstract unity of thought, and as that which deviates from it, constitute[s] the variety found in the world of sense. . . . In this way the concrete complex of material things is isolated from Spirit, and presented in wild distraction, except as re-absorbed in the pure ideality of Brahman" (PH 156). In the absence of a world lacking real substance or being, however, the Absolute cannot recognize itself. The Indian religious consciousness "presents a union of the natural and spiritual, in which nature, on the one hand, does not present itself as a world embodying Reason, nor the spiritual, on the other hand, as consciousness in contrast with nature" (PH 161). Consequently, the divine can never attain the self-knowledge or self-consciousness toward which it strives. It remains a formless, abstract entity—"intellection itself in its greatest vacuity" (PH 156). Hence, the Oriental world with its nature religions must be superseded by another phase of world history: the world of Greece and Rome and its correlative spiritual principle.

In Hegel's scheme of world history, the second major period encompasses the ancient Greco-Roman world. This historical phase also includes, in addition to the religions associated with Greece and Rome, the religious heritage of Judaism. In his *Vorlesungen über die Philosophie der Geschichte*, Hegel discusses the Jewish faith in the context of the Oriental world. It is clear from his analysis of Judaism in the *Lectures on the Philosophy of Religion*, however, that its rightful place in the course of world history is as part of the Greco-Roman world. As the initial manifestation of the religion which elevates the spiritual above the natural, Judaism introduces a religious principle that is antithetical to the basic theological precepts of Eastern religion and whose development continues in the sphere of Greek religiosity.

According to Hegel's analysis of the progressive advance of the religious consciousness, the religions of Judea and of Hellas are joined together by a common feature: the emergent view of God as an independent spiritual or individual personality, rather than an entity totally immersed in, and identical to, the world of nature. At this phase of religious evolution, "the spiritual develops itself in sharp contrast to nature and to union with it" (PH 195). This movement beyond the naturalistic basis of earlier world religions is expressed most sharply in the religion of Judaism (which Hegel designates as the religion of sublimity). In contrast to the monistic worldview of the Oriental religious traditions, the Jewish religion is characterized by an unmistakable dualism. The essential unity of the spiritual and the natural is rent apart, and replaced by a view of God as a spiritual reality which exists above and beyond the material world. "The spiritual God of the Jews arrests our attention—like Brahman, existing only for thought, yet [unlike Brahman] jealous and excluding from his being and abolishing all distinct speciality of manifestations, such as are freely allowed in other religions" (PH 114). In contrast to the nature religions, the Jewish faith conceives God not as a principle immanent within the world, but as a sublime and transcendent subject which, as such, is Lord of nature and history. The divine reality is thereby differentiated from, and external to, the natural order. In relation to God, the status and value of the latter are de minimis (as witnessed to by the Hebraic view of creation ex nihilo). The world is not intrinsically connected to the divine, although it constitutes a realm of being which is more than illusory, and, as such, stands over against the divine Lord. "This forms the point of separation between the East and the West; Spirit descends into the depths of its own being, and recognizes the abstract fundamental principle as the spiritual. Nature—which in the East is the primary and fundamental existence—is now depressed to the condition of a mere creature; and Spirit now occupies the first place. God is known as the creator of all men, as he is of all nature, and as absolute causality generally" (PH 195).

From Hegel's perspective, however, the advance in the evolution of religious consciousness represented by the Jewish faith is a mixed blessing. The notion of God as a discrete, spiritual individual no longer totally immersed in natural processes is a noteworthy achievement. But the gains wrought by this development are ultimately offset by the costs which it entails. The result of the complete separation of God and world is Spirit's inability to recognize itself in the domain of finitude. The latter appears to it as an altogether alien object, and not in any way as its own product.

In the face of the radical antithesis between God and world found in Judaism, a countertrend emerged in the Greek world. An attempt was made to reunite these seemingly opposed spheres while retaining the vision of God as subject found in the Jewish tradition. Greek religion accomplished this primarily by means of its essential anthropomorphism, in which the unity of the spiritual and the natural is reestablished. This reunification occurs, however, exclusively in human shape and not in the form of purely natural entities (as in the religions of nature).

> It must be further observed, that the Greek gods are to be regarded as individualities—not abstractions, like "Knowledge," "Unity," "Time," "Heaven," "Necessity." Such abstractions do not form the substance of these divinities; they are no allegories, no abstract beings, to which various attributes are attached. . . . [On the contrary, t]he gods are personalities, concrete individualities. [PH 246]

> While they each have an individual character, the Greek gods are also represented as human, and this anthropomorphism is charged as a defect. On the contrary (we may immediately rejoin) man as the spiritual constitutes the element of truth in the Greek gods that rendered them superior to all elemental deities, and all mere abstractions of the One and Highest Being. [PH 248]

By envisioning divine reality in the guise of genuine human persons, a tentative reconciliation between the Infinite and the finite thereby occurs. The latter is seen as an aspect of God. The former is again seen as manifesting itself through nature. This rapprochement is most tangibly presented in the visual art characteristic of Greek religion, from which Hegel derives the category of the religion of beauty. In a lengthy passage, Hegel vividly describes the newly found intimate relation between the spiritual and the natural that is paramount in the religion of Greece:

> In summing up the constituents of the *Greek spirit*, we find its fundamental characteristic to be, that the freedom of Spirit is conditioned by and has an essential relation to some stimulus supplied by nature. . . . The Greek spirit as the medium between the two, begins with nature, but transforms it into a mere objective form of its (Spirit's) own existence; . . . This stamps the Greek character as that of *individuality conditioned by beauty*, which is produced by Spirit, transforming the merely natural into an expression of its own being. The activity of Spirit does not yet possess in itself the material and organ of expression, but needs the excitement of nature and

the matter which nature supplies: it is not free, self-determining spirituality, but merely naturalness formed to spirituality—Spiritual Individuality. The Greek spirit is the plastic artist, forming the stone into a work of art. In this formative process the stone does not remain mere stone—the form being only superinduced from without; but it is made an expression of the spiritual, even contrary to its nature, and thus transformed. Conversely, the artist *needs* for his spiritual conceptions, stone, colors, sensuous forms to express his idea. Without such an element he can no more be conscious of the idea himself, than give it an objective form for the contemplation of others; since it cannot in thought alone become an object to him. . . . In Greek beauty the sensuous is only a sign, an expression, an envelope, in which Spirit manifests itself. [PH 238–39]

Thus, the emergence of God's status as a spiritual individual, won by the religion of Judaism, is preserved in the religion of the Greeks, but in such a way that Spirit is seen as embodied in the natural, rather than as totally opposed to nature. The apparent synthesis of God and world which Greek religion achieves, however, is itself inadequate. As reflected in its characteristic polytheism, the numerous Olympian deities of the Greek pantheon are themselves only limited, parochial divinities. Each possesses only partial (and not absolute) power—much unlike the universal, all-powerful God of Abraham et al. "That higher thought, the knowledge of unity as God—the One Spirit—lay beyond that grade of thought which the Greeks had attained" (PH 246). "It must be observed, that the divinity of the Greeks is not yet the *absolute,* free Spirit, but Spirit in a particular mode, fettered by the limitations of humanity—still dependent as a determinate individuality on external conditions. Individualities, objectively beautiful, are the gods of the Greeks" (PH 244). For Hegel Greek religion represents a significant advance beyond the harsh antitheses of the Jewish faith and toward the final reconciliation of God and world. However, it, too, must eventually be superseded.[17]

In Hegel's vision of world history, the emergence of Christianity—the dominant spiritual force of the Germanic (or Western European) world—represents the apex of religious development and so deserves the appellation of the consummate (or absolute) religion. The appearance of the Christian religion within the theater of world history marks the apprehension of the true nature of God and the final reconciliation of God and world. "The recognition of the identity of the subject and God was introduced into the World when *the fullness of time was come:* the consciousness of this identity is the recognition of God in his true essence" (PH 323). Through its central doctrine of the Incarnation, which posits that the divine and human are united in the particular figure of Jesus Christ, the ultimate truth about God's nature and being is finally revealed to humanity. By means of the doctrine of the God-Man, Christianity holds that the Infinite and the finite are essentially one. At the same time, the differences between them are not abolished. *"Christ has appeared—a man who is God—God who is man; and thereby peace and reconciliation have accrued to the world"* (PH 324). Thus, according to Hegel, religious development reaches a perfect and complete culmination with the Christian religion. Christianity must itself undergo a gradual and multiphased process of internal development, in which its symbolic presentation of the truth is translated into the more adequate conceptual language of philosophy. But for Hegel the Christian religion represents the pinnacle of religious history. The significance of the Christian religion is "absolutely epoch-making" (LPH 40). Indeed, it provides nothing less than "the key to world history" (LPH 41), and, as such, represents the perfect fulfillment of the divine Spirit's ultimate goals and purposes.[18]

Hegel's philosophy of history—like other paradigmatic fictions in the history of Western ideas—has met a curious fate over the decades and even centuries since its inception. In the wake of Hegel's own intellectual career, we may trace a continuing preoccupation with the Hegelian paradigm on the part of numerous post-Hegelian thinkers of various persuasions, ranging from the critical sociology of Karl Marx to the philosophico-theological reflection of Søren Kierkegaard, to the analytical school of the philosophy of history. In each case we may discern the attempt to make sense of the way Hegel tried to make sense of life. Such attempts are strikingly original to the thinker in question, yet highly derivative from Hegel's own imaginative vision. Thus, the course of intellectual history since Hegel discloses both the growing obsolescence of the Hegelian paradigm, as later thinkers criticized and renounced many of its essential principles, and, paradoxically, its stubborn persistence over time, as these same critics assimilated many of its features.

Among these interpretations of the Hegelian paradigm of history is that of Ernst Troeltsch. His achievement may be defined, at least in part, as an attempt to understand historical experience by coming to terms with this particular precedent of sense-making in Western thought. The remaining chapters of this essay track Troeltsch's critical appropriation of the Hegelian paradigm over the course of his wide-ranging intellectual career. In them I argue for the thesis that, in important ways, Troeltsch's thought embodies a gradual movement away from the simplicity of the Hegelian paradigm, as well as a continuing relationship to it. In chapter 3, I analyze the Hegelian presence in Troeltsch's early essays regarding the status of religion in the modern world.

The Crisis of Religion in the Modern World:
The Influence of Hegel in Troeltsch's Early Writings

The Fate of Religion in the Modern World

"Gentlemen, everything is tottering!"[1] With this bold assertion, Ernst Troeltsch began his remarks before the 1896 assembly of "die Freunde der Christlichen Welt," held in Eisenach, Germany. Troeltsch's perception that the ground was figuratively quaking beneath his feet was not, of course, unique to him. A widely diffused sense of crisis existed, even flourished, within certain intellectual circles in the West as the nineteenth century approached its close.[2] His special contribution to such fin-de-siècle trepidation, however, was to probe into the major causes of this anxiety within the modern framework of religious life. For Troeltsch, the age in which he lived was a preeminent turning point in the spiritual history of Western civilization. It was a juncture teeming with possibilities generated by novel and provocative secular modes of thought and a moment simultaneously faltering under the weight of the seemingly moribund beliefs, values, and institutions of Western religion. As a result, many observers judged traditional religion to be at the end of an era, its future uncertain as it was buffeted by onrushing ideational currents. Responding to this profound spiritual emergency, Troeltsch defined his own task as twofold. First he chose to investigate and clarify the most significant new systems of knowledge and philosophical movements responsible for this predicament. This project served, in turn, as a prelude to his efforts to reestablish some terra firma upon which modern individuals might found a religious worldview and construct a religious ethic.

In "Die christliche Weltanschauung und ihre Gegenströmungen," Troeltsch elaborates upon the fundamental cause of the spiritual malaise facing humanity in the late nineteenth century. This dilemma was rooted in the "irreconcilable conflict" (GS 2:229) between a series of compelling intellectual forces that had arisen from different quarters in the modern world and the centuries-old religious beliefs of the Christian heritage. "Since the new science won over the hearts of those sick and tired of religious dispute following the religious wars, and since the great cultural upheaval of the seventeenth and eighteenth centuries began, great currents of thought have emerged which carried with them altogether new facts and observations and which presented the Christian faith with an overwhelming abundance of new problems" (GS 2:229–30).

Two important factors further underscored the gravity of this state of affairs. On the one hand, the most prominent countercurrents of modernity could hardly be dismissed as the idiosyncratic products of solitary thinkers or as restrictive theoretical accounts confined to relatively incidental data within human experience. On the contrary, the revolutionary new scientific and philosophical systems then at hand represented "universal currents of world literature . . . the movement of modern life itself" (GS 2:238). They provided coherent and holistic interpretations of human, natural, and social reality. Indeed, by addressing the central problems of self, nature, and society, these diverse worldviews, each in its own way, attempted both to raise and to answer humanity's most serious existential questions. As such, they stood, at least in the minds of free thinkers, as genuine alternatives to the view of life proffered by the Christian tradition.

On the other hand, the most penetrating intellectual movements of modernity imperiled not merely selected doctrines of the Christian faith that believers might strategically concede in order to retain the truth of Christianity overall. Rather, "the entire network of Christianity, the Christian worldview as a whole, is called into question, not a particular precept" (GS 2:239). Indeed, at stake in the confrontation between modern culture and Christian faith was nothing less than the latter's most fundamental tenets regarding the quintessential religious themes of God, self, and world (and the interrelationship among these *Grundideen*). "It is a question . . . for theology of all gradations, whether the entirety of its ethical-religious view of God, world, and man can co-exist with the new groups of facts advancing on our horizon, or whether their irreconcilability must drive us to the procurement of another worldview, to the hope in a new religion" (GS 2:239). Many of Troeltsch's theological contemporaries regarded the truth and integrity of the Christian worldview and its concomitant inner experience of salvation as self-evident. But Troeltsch himself did not dispute that the validity of Christianity as a bona fide spiritual principle was itself in doubt—a fact which others could ignore only at their own risk. This opposition between modern consciousness and religious faith generated a spiritual crisis that reached to the depths of the Christian religion. For Troeltsch at least, its outcome was genuinely in doubt. "Here begins the abundantly painful religious crisis in the midst of which we find ourselves. We are unable to say how indeed it will end. About it we can say only—that it struggles towards a harmonization of science and religion" (GS 2:230).

In the face of this critical situation, Troeltsch rejected mere declarations of hostility toward modernity. Instead, he assumed the theologian's perennial task of reconciling Christian religiosity and the most relevant signs of the times of the secular world. Such a modus vivendi was accomplished with relative ease and success by earlier generations. This task was now much more problematic because of the radical disjunction between *Wissenschaft* and *Glaube*.[3] Troeltsch's point of departure in "Die christliche Weltanschauung" was to identify and characterize the most important intellectual trends in the West since the dawn of the Enlightenment: natural science, neohumanism, and positivism.[4] Both individually and collectively, these movements of thought challenged to the utmost the continued survival of the Christian *Lebensanschauung*.

Natural Science

In Troeltsch's mind, the most dominant of the great countercurrents of modernity in its influence on the then-contemporary worldview was natural science. Natural science prescribes the application of a set of rigorously defined methodological principles to the study of the physical world, in pursuit of increasingly more adequate knowledge of that world. As embodied in the pioneering work of Isaac Newton, the fledgling scientific method was based on (1) the observation and description of all relevant events, entities, and processes found in nature in a manner faithful to the empirically available evidence, such that (2) the various laws and theoretical models by which such data were understood might be inductively derived. Over time, the systematic prosecution of such inquiry by innumerable investigators led to the eclipse of the science of antiquity and the emergence of far-reaching developments in various fields. In physics, astronomy, and chemistry the laws which govern matter and energy, the movement of the celestial bodies, and the composition and transformation of physical entities were formulated as hypotheses, tested by experimentation, and ultimately verified. Of greater significance, however, was the rise, upon the foundation of these diverse results, of a singular vision of the "universe governed by means of uniform, mathematical-mechanical laws" (GS 2:230). All of reality, "from the large-scale movements of the heavenly bodies to the most minute physiological events," was seen as "an entirely closed, self-contained network" (GS 2:241). Its multiple phenomena were regulated by a set of universal and immutable laws capable of mathematically precise articulation, such as the Newtonian laws of motion, the law of conservation of matter and energy, and the laws of thermodynamics. From this perspective, nothing happens in the world either by chance or by the impingement of forces which are somehow outside or beyond nature. Nature is an uninterrupted concatenation of objects and processes, the functioning and interaction of which can be rationally explained and calculated in terms of laws immanent to the world itself.

The emergence of this *Weltanschauung* had immediate repercussions for traditional Christian beliefs regarding the relationship of the natural and supernatural orders. In particular, it affected the modern understanding of God's relation to the realm of nature, as this relationship is reflected in the classical theological doctrines of providence and creation. The Newtonian picture of the world as a perfect machine, perhaps created and set in motion by God as its First Cause but certainly requiring no further divine interference, rendered questionable the Christian understanding of God's continuing intervention in the cosmic order. Indeed, the persistent affirmation of the fundamental regularity of the natural world established by the various *Naturwissenschaften* eventually seemed altogether to preclude the sort of divine activity upon which centuries of Christian faith had been based. The conception of nature as a self-perpetuating and self-sufficient system governed by laws inherent within the cosmos led to the conclusion that a transcendent creator was no longer required, either to start the world going or to inscribe the laws of nature within the universe by an act of divine volition. Thus, by establishing and heightening an awareness of "the homogeneity and the indissoluble lawful interconnection of Nature," modern scientific inquiry dealt "a heavy blow to the naive biblical-ecclesiastical supernaturalism" (GS 2:230) which provided the framework for the aforementioned articles of belief.[5]

The natural sciences promoted a vision of the world as a law-regulated mechanism that fostered an understanding of the structure and dynamics of the universe in nontheological terms. However, other principles intended to account for its substance led to results equally unpalatable to Christianity. The retrieval of the ancient doctrine of atomism, occasioned by various scientific discoveries since the seventeenth century, invariably implied a monistic materialist ontology. This ontology contrasted with the supernatural dualism on which the Christian understanding of God and self (or the relationship between spirit and nature) is founded. The rise to prominence of atomistic explanations of the physical world engendered the theory that the universe is composed of simple and uniform elements of an essentially homogeneous nature. Its fundamental stuff consists of just one kind of substance—matter and its various combinations and permutations. Accordingly, primary ontological status was ascribed to material essence, and all other ostensibly nonmaterial spheres of reality were regarded as secondary, as in some manner derivative from, or dependent on, this material core. The drift of thought stimulated by atomistic theory "pushed forward to the complete reduction of all occurrences to mathematical-mechanical movement, and so to the purely empirical treatment, analogous to natural science, even of psychical phenomena. Thus arose from this propensity of thought . . . the [doctrine of] pure materialism, which dissolved even the life of the spirit in atomistic-mechanistic movement" (GS 2:231).

From this perspective, certain basic theological and anthropological assertions of the Christian tradition, "with its positive valuation of spiritual and personal life" (GS 2:247), were shown to be vulnerable, as materialistic theory attempted "to explain the more refined physiological and biological, as well as psychological occurrences, by use of its methods" (GS 2:231). Proponents of materialism tended to account for our so-called higher activity, such as thought, memory, and personality, completely in terms of organic causes and stimuli common to all physical reality. This deprived the spiritual dimension of human existence of its uniqueness and autonomy and denied as well that we possess an incorporeal, immortal soul. The life of the spirit was regarded merely as "a side-effect, an accompanying phenomenon, of the process of nature," and not as the "more sublime type of reality" (GS 2:248) posited by Christianity. Furthermore, by extrapolation, the materialist view also rendered inadmissible the existence of all supernatural beings who ostensibly possess certain psychological properties (for example, consciousness or will), but who do not subsist in material form. As a result, the objective reality of God, at least insofar as God is conceived as a spiritual entity, was seriously undermined. It thereby became "the conviction of all persons educated in the natural sciences that, whatever the case may be with the spiritual world, every supernatural dualism is forever impossible; and many assume, in addition, since nature alone is that which is certain and perceptible, that 'spirit' is therefore at the very least something quite problematic" (GS 2:231).

Thus, for Troeltsch, the rise of natural science, and especially the worldview and primary metaphysical assumptions latent in its concept of nature, led to potentially devastating conclusions for some of Christianity's most crucial doctrines. In a dramatic way, the essential tenets of the Christian faith encountered an alternative Weltanschauung that was grounded on the data of natural reality and that had achieved considerable intellectual respectability since its origins in the seventeenth and eighteenth centuries. But if Christianity found itself susceptible to an attack from disciplines originating from an investigation of nature, its confrontation with the second countercurrent of modernity discussed by Troeltsch yielded results that were equally problematic. This latter thought-world was set in motion by an appreciation of the most splendid cultural creations of humanity.

Neohumanism

The second major countercurrent that Troeltsch treats in his brief review of modern intellectual history is neohumanism. The historical roots of this Weltanschauung are found in the Hellenistic art and culture of antiquity and of the Renaissance. It only came to fruition, however, during the late eighteenth and early nineteenth centuries in Western Europe, primarily in Germany and England. In part a direct response to the worldview espoused by the scientists and *philosophes* of the Age of Enlightenment, the neohumanist movement generated an alternative conception of the universe that was articulated in terms both of a distinctive aesthetic sensibility and a unique philosophical vision.

The artistic and literary creations of Goethe, the Schlegels, and Coleridge, and the idealist philosophy of Fichte, Schelling, and especially the "gargantuan work" (GS 2:232) of Hegel, all shared a common devotion to the tenets of organicism. These thinkers regarded the world as an integrated totality, based on the model of a living organism. Parts within the whole are interrelated in a dialectical fashion, and differences among seemingly opposed phenomena are more apparent than real.

> The speculative notion of "the beautiful" as the inner unity of spirit and nature in a living organism reconciles the inert masses of mechanical-mathematical nature with the inner vitality of spirit, the infinite profusion of individual existence with the unity of a whole. In the employment of Kantian thought, nature appears as the expression, as the reverse side of spirit. The aesthetic gaze at the active whole of the natural world again discerns everywhere in various combinations the same identity of spirit and nature, which to us appears in a distinctive way only in human reality. [GS 2:232][6]

Neohumanists, therefore, did not consider God and world as independent, mutually exclusive realities, as did certain proponents of the Enlightenment. Adopting a so-called deistic view, the latter saw nature as a machine created by a transcendent God (who remains outside of the world) and ruled by unchanging, impersonal laws. In contrast, neohumanists envisioned the cosmos not as a mechanism but as a vital, living body, infused and animated by the divine power immanent within it. According to the basic principles of neohumanist thought, God and world interpenetrate in the closest possible way. Nature is the self-expression or embodiment of the divine Spirit, while God dwells intimately within the universe as its creative source and ground:

> The totality of nature is ensouled and is a uniform, living cosmos, the All—the active divine nature—moving rhythmically according to the law of beauty. For this reason, the emphasis falls less on classifying the mechanical regularity of nature in the living cosmos than on demonstrating the uniform life of spirit in history, unfolding itself in gradual stages, in which the spirit, still slumbering in nature, for the first time awakens to full life. Indeed, the mechanistic view of nature is altogether overcome and replaced by means of a poetical, historical-developmental theory of the materialization of spirit and the increasing spiritualization of matter. [GS 2:232–33]

The "aesthetic monism" (GS 2:233) which Troeltsch regarded as a primary feature of neohumanism also conflicted directly with the dualism characteristic of biblical-ecclesiastical supernaturalism. "Contrary to the Christian dualism of God and world to which faith attests . . . the radiant belief in the unity of the world and of life in itself emerges" (GS 2:234).[7] Despite the tendency even within Christian orthodoxy to regard God as in some way both transcendent to, and immanent within, the natural order, traditional Christianity has consistently affirmed the fundamental ontological difference between God and world.[8] This affirmation, however, was confronted by the explicitly pantheistic conception of God characteristic of neohumanism. Reminiscent of the challenge posed by materialism, the fundamental distinction between God and world, or spirit and matter, collapsed in the face of neohumanism's monistic vision, once again endangering the more conventional theistic beliefs of Christianity. Whether by reducing life's spiritual dimension to the realm of matter, as the doctrine of philosophical materialism associated with the *Naturwissenschaften* proposed, or by asserting the underlying identity of spirit and matter, as did neohumanism, the "absolute monism" (GS 2:247) of both currents of thought threatened the essential dualism on which traditional Christian faith was based.

By all accounts, the impact of the neohumanist movement on the

Western cultural scene was explosive. Nevertheless, even in its most mature form, neohumanism was a relatively fleeting phenomenon, enjoying a lifetime of only several decades. Its unifying worldview eventually succumbed to the transvaluation of its central values. As embodied in the thought of a transitional figure such as Schopenhauer, the many virtues of the neohumanist outlook on life—its confidence in human reason and knowledge, its pervasive optimism, its sense of the harmony and beauty of the cosmos—were gradually dispelled. In turn, neohumanism was replaced by ostensibly more sober and realistic, if philosophically less ambitious, movements of thought. These included its most influential successor, positivism.

Positivism

The third and final countercurrent of modernity which Troeltsch discusses in "Die christliche Weltanschauung" is positivism. Positivism arose in the wake of the dissolution of the neohumanist synthesis and grew to prominence during a period roughly coterminous with Troeltsch's own lifespan. Despite its internal diversity, as exemplified by the thought of such proponents as Auguste Comte, Herbert Spencer, and John Stuart Mill, the common thread of the positivist movement is the shared epistemological stance from which its name is derived. For this school of thought, positive facts alone are possible objects of knowledge, and such facts are only cognizable by means of science and its methods. In antipathy to the alleged flights of metaphysical speculation typical of both materialism and neohumanism, positivism self-consciously restricted itself to knowledge of what is directly accessible to the knower. It adopted, therefore, an attitude of unabashed scepticism regarding the knowability of the ultimate causes, essences, or ideas ostensibly underlying human and natural reality, instead relying exclusively on "knowledge and mastery of the positive data" (GS 2:247).

Positivism's embrace of "two vigorous fundamental ideas" (GS 2:236), however, led to consequences detrimental to certain traditional Christian beliefs. These were a biologically based notion of evolution and a utilitarian theory of social ethics. Many positivist thinkers (especially Spencer) looked to the theory of evolution to account for the progressive unfolding of the universe, from the cosmic nebula to "the mysteries of organic and historical life" (GS 2:236). From this perspective, a seemingly endless evolutionary process has moved inexorably forward according to certain natural laws. These laws regulate the emergence and development of both inanimate and animate entities, including the highest forms of life. Informed by the observations and theories of Charles Darwin, the positivists explained the continual evolution of the varieties of organic life in terms of the mechanism of natural selection. Those species most adaptable to their environment in the struggle for life tend to endure and reproduce, and they transmit to their progeny those characteristics most suited to survival. Life forms whose response to their milieu is maladaptive become hereditarily less equipped for survival and ultimately disappear.

As a result of evolution theory, the longstanding religious claim for the special status of humanity as somehow qualitatively separated from the rest of the natural order was subjected to a radical critique. From the positivist perspective, "every possession of the spirit, apparently self-validating, has thus arisen as a product of outside forces, and will be changed further by these forces, according to fixed laws of mass-movement" (GS 2:236). The intimate link of homo sapiens with its animal ancestors was thereby exposed. Now the center and crown of creation, humankind may in turn be dethroned by more highly evolved variants of life that promise to arise in the future sweep of evolutionary history.

Despite its sense of our deep immersion in natural processes, however, positivism nevertheless allowed for human intelligence and reason. This vestige of dignity and worth blatantly contradicts the forces of "unreason" characteristic of the world-at-large and "forms the one 'element' of rationality amidst the great surrounding chaos" (GS 2:236). Indeed, "the capacity of reason characteristic of the human species is the only significant thing, the only intelligible point in the universal, restless process of evolution. It walks in the path trod earlier by the divine" (GS 2:237). Under these circumstances, it is our task pragmatically to apply knowledge of the laws of nature and of life itself so as to ensure the survival of humanity and the improvement of its lot. Defined in ethical terms, it is our duty to promote societal welfare by maximizing the collective well-being of the human community. For this intelligence, according to the positivists, "grows the task scientifically to calculate its actual and potential goals . . . and to accomplish them clearly, soberly, and certainly, with all of the strength of an undivided will of the species, in prudent adaptation to nature" (GS 2:237). In keeping with its maxim to limit ourselves to what is objectively given, the advocates of positivism thus endorse a teleological (or purely immanent) social ethic. The notion of the good is conceived in concrete, this-worldly terms. Primary emphasis is placed on the responsible solution of mundane economic and social problems. This strikingly utilitarian concept of the good, defined as the greatest possible happiness of the greatest number of people, sharply opposes traditional philosophical and religious views of morality. In particular, certain positivists evinced complete disdain toward all "transcendent motives and goals" (GS 2:235), including both Kant's categorical imperative and the Christian vision of "other-worldly blessedness" (GS 2:237). These critics regarded the religious definition of the proper end of ethical conduct as especially illusory. In their eyes, it is founded upon the equally dubious notion of a just and beneficent God, whose function in the moral universe is primarily to "make good again what has been neglected and complete all that is deficient" (GS 2:237). From the perspective of positivism, humanity's ultimate task is to liberate itself from the childish fantasies of a religiously based morality that ignores the "inexorable limits of the natural world" (GS 2:235). Instead we must firmly ground our moral theory and practice exclusively in the pragmatic solution of inner-worldly problems.

The Autonomy of Religion and Its Scientific Treatment

Each of the major countercurrents of the modern world which Troeltsch considers at the outset of "Die christliche Weltanschauung" provides a distinctive, but equally formidable, challenge to the essential beliefs of the Christian religion. Whatever differences may exist among them, however, the final result of the assault which they launched is clear: Christianity was caught in a hostile crossfire of thought-currents which threatened its survival. But Troeltsch was also haunted by the specter of the dissolution of all religious forms in the wake of this modern crisis. He therefore shifted from the relatively unsystematic counterattack in the name of the Christian religion found in "Die christliche Weltanschauung" to a concerted attempt, in a series of later essays written during the first decade of his academic career, to validate the elementary forms of religious life in general. This constructive effort was designed as a more comprehensive response to the counterclaims previously considered and was intended ultimately to lead to the rejuvenation and reshaping of the basic doctrines of Christianity. Troeltsch endeavored to execute this task by formulating the essential principles of a science of religion, whereby the relative independence of religious experience might be affirmed. In so doing, Troeltsch retained certain features of the Hegelian paradigm as one of the cornerstones upon which his own scientific reflection on religion was based.

The Idealistic Presupposition

In "Wesen der Religion und der Religionswissenschaft,"[9] Troeltsch presents a methodological overview of the science of religion. For Troeltsch, the scientific treatment of religion is not presupposition-less. One must first choose the basic philosophical perspective from which to investigate the subject. Its proper execution depends upon the self-conscious adoption of an appropriate overarching stance whose assumptions then regulate all subsequent inquiry into the religious data. This decision, Troeltsch felt, may properly be confined to a choice between two mutually contradictory philosophical points of view: idealism and positivism. Only between these two philosophical foundations is a decision possible regarding the most viable interpretation of "the great cultural creations of the human mind" (RSR 82).[10] Idealism regards these phenomena as the spontaneous creations of human reason. Their autonomy is guaranteed by the irreducible and unconditional quality of that mental reality which generates the diverse spiritual ideas and values of humankind from its own mysterious depths.[11] In contrast, positivism espouses a less generous view of the nature and function of mind. Its adherents posit that reason is not endowed with the qualitatively creative impulses that idealism attributes to it. Rather, it is "nothing more than the formal power to shape a system of generalisations out of positive facts as far as possible objectively conceived, and to make this system serve the aims of human survival and the advancement of the race. . . . We have above all the regular and homogeneous linkage of the objective facts of the external world, and in the inward world no mystery other than the ability to recognize the laws of nature and to use them for maintaining the life of the species" (RSR 82). From this point of view, the ideals and values of the human species, as embodied in phenomena such as religion, are ultimately divorced from their alleged ontological grounding in human cognitive powers. Hence, they must be reinterpreted in terms of explanatory principles different from those that philosophical idealism offers.

A choice between these two fundamental options, in Troeltsch's view, is thus required in order to initiate any scientific inquiry into religion. His personal investigation into the data of religion presupposes the idealist philosophical standpoint, while he unequivocally rejects that of positivism. This choice has its obvious benefits. Positivism denies the truth of religion and seeks to explain its origin and function strictly as a psychologically motivated illusion. Idealism, in contrast, grants the possibility (at least in principle) that religion is an autonomous sphere of reality and not the epiphenomenal product of more elemental psychic or societal forces. It thereby respects the contentions which the religious consciousness makes for itself regarding its independent status in the world. "The way must be held open for religion to be fully apprehended. It must be possible to analyze it in its own terms. It must be examined at least provisionally as a completely independent phenomenon, which it claims itself after all to be. It must not be made subject from the start to general theories which prescribe in a prejudicial way what in religion is justifiable and what is not" (RSR 85). Accordingly, Troeltsch prefers the perspective of idealism because it does not offer a preconceived interpretation of religion. Instead, it allows for a bias-free analysis of the religious data, in which religion is allowed to speak for itself. Indeed, in Troeltsch's view, only in this way can true knowledge of "religion as it really is"(RSR 92) be attained.

Troeltsch's preliminary decision in favor of idealism, of course, is only the first step in the science of religion which he articulates. Its actual implementation requires that investigators employ their descriptive and analytical tools in the examination of religion as it is actually found in human experience. Thus, in direct contrast to the procedures of pre-Enlightenment philosophy of religion, which attempted scientifically to validate the religious object, Troeltsch endorsed the crucial methodological shift within post-Kantian scientific inquiry into religion. This shift directed attention away "from the attempt at a metaphysical determination of religious objects or of the idea of God" (RSR 111) and toward "the most essential and leading [religious] phenomena" (RSR 92) within human life itself.

"Ever since, there has been only one philosophy of religion. It is not a philosophical treatment of the objects of religion, but rather a treatment of religion itself as an independent, self-coherent area of life, evolving according to fixed laws" (SR 368).

Upon further examination, such an analysis discloses that "real, living religion" (SR 377), despite the immense diversity of religious data, characteristically manifests itself in discrete realms within the compass of human experience. As identified by significant sectors of nineteenth-century thought, the two primary loci of religion are human consciousness and the world of reality external to the mind, constituted primarily by the realms of history and culture. "The sensitivity of recent thought to everything factual, concrete and empirical, has steered research emphatically towards the examination of religious phenomena as these are available in the realm of historical, psychological reality" (RSR 86–87). The fundamental task of the new science of religion, therefore, is to explore the religious dimension of reality along the two basic routes identified by the century-long investigation of religion which preceded Troeltsch's own involvement in this field. These two avenues are (1) the turn to the subject, and (2) the turn to history. They provide the heuristic categories according to which Troeltsch's particular contribution to the science of religion, as well as his appeal to the Hegelian paradigm, may be clarified and understood.

The Turn to the Subject

In the modern period of Western religious thought, the methodological moment that I designate as the turn to the subject was indeed a central characteristic of religious inquiry. Investigators into the nature and meaning of human religiosity carefully probed the depths and recesses of human subjectivity as a central component of their study of religion, in order to analyze and explicate, as accurately and rigorously as possible, the phenomenon of religion. As part of this general trend, scientific inquiry into the relationship between forms of religion and our inner world took various shapes, in keeping with the aims and predilections of the investigator. Thus, a survey of the efforts during the nineteenth century to explore the subjective character of religious experience reveals the intimate link of religion with moral consciousness (Kant), rational consciousness (Hegel), human volition (Kierkegaard), and the affective element within human experience (Schleiermacher). Nevertheless, despite the obvious diversity among these seminal thinkers, all shared the firm conviction that human religiosity is localized (at least in part) in the subjective workings of human beings. Hence, each in his own way strove methodically to examine the structure and dynamics of consciousness in order more adequately to understand the uniquely religious dimension of human life.

Following their lead, Troeltsch also appropriated the subjective turn in his own scientific treatment of religion. In Troeltsch's case, however, his formal conformity to the turn to the subject took precise material shape in his pursuit of the different but related enterprises of the psychology of religion and epistemology. Each was part of his effort to come to terms with religion as a datum of inner experience.

THE PSYCHOLOGY OF RELIGION

As Troeltsch queries in "Die Selbständigkeit der Religion," "What does the psychology of religion prove? What is religion itself, whose mode of treatment has up to now only been spoken about in its most general psychical manifestation?" (SR 380). According to Troeltsch, the main purpose of the psychological analysis of religious phenomena is to study the religious life of humanity as it is grounded in our mental activities. Pursuant to the general methodological considerations discussed above, this task does not try to explain religion as a secondary by-product of other, more fundamental psychological processes, as certain positivist critics of religion would prefer to do. Rather than raise the question of the genesis or psychological origin of religion, the psychology of religion accepts the subjective religious data as given and irreducible facts of human psychic life. It thereby strives empathically to enter into the religious consciousness itself. Either by self-observation (where the scientific researcher possesses adequate religious sensibilities) or by listening in on the inner life of especially religious persons as reported by these individuals, it is possible accurately and objectively to describe the most typical characteristics of subjective religiosity. "The first task [of the psychology of religion] must be to grasp the phenomenon as far as possible in its naivety, to win from it the experience or outlook as yet uninfluenced by scientific interpretation. This was already marked out above as the starting point of a scientific treatment

of religion. At this point of identification psychology begins"
(RSR 114).

Despite the rampant variety to be found there, Troeltsch suggests
that certain outstanding features of religion as a psychological fact
may be identified and catalogued by such a phenomenological
method of analysis. Most significantly, the primary content which
may be so observed is the subjective reality of faith in the dynamic
presence of the divine, even as the deity is variably conceived within
different religious traditions. In turn, "the mental representation of
superhuman . . . powers and realities" (SR 381) is often accompanied by the inner experience, in some fashion, of the divine reality
itself. This experience assumes different modes, including the experience of a communication initiated by the divine (in the form of
revelation or enlightenment), or of a direct relationship or inner
connection with the deity (especially via the mystical union of the
finite with the Infinite). Indeed, the prevalence of the latter type of
experience within virtually all of the great religious traditions leads
Troeltsch to identify mysticism as the psychological religious datum
par excellence, as "the primary phenomenon of all religion" (RSR
115). He also observed that within the realm of subjective religiosity, these types of personal religious experiences are generally
accompanied by a wide array of specifically religious moods and
feelings. "The linkage of mental images with certain accompanying
feelings" (SR 380) is a fundamental feature of the religious consciousness, as it is of consciousness in general. These impulses are
determined and affected by the particular manner in which the religious individual experiences the divine, and include such classical
religious emotions as awe, rapture, reverence, exaltation, bliss,
serenity, and even fear or horror. Finally, a cluster of different pos-
tures of psychological attentiveness are characteristically associated
with inward religious experience and may be identified in the course
of such an investigation (for example, prayer, meditation, prophecy,
and devotion).

EPISTEMOLOGY

If the basic task of the psychology of religion is successfully to provide an unbiased depiction of the inner events of religious life as they
are present in the minds of religious individuals, how can we ascertain the truth of these ideas and experiences? What is the cognitive

import of the religious ideas disclosed by a purely psychological analysis of subjective religious experience? As long as one remains within the framework of empirical description, according to Troeltsch, the truth-status of subjective religiosity remains an unanswered and indeed an unanswerable question. The psychology of religion, while adequate to its assignment, is a necessary but insufficient approach within the larger investigation into the validity of intrapersonal religious phenomena. In order to determine the validity of these phenomena, the scientific examination of religion must prescind from the methodologically delimited purpose of psychological observation and undertake an epistemological analysis of human consciousness in general and the epistemic status of religious ideas in particular. Within Troeltsch's schema of the science of religion, the subjective turn inaugurated by the psychology of religion must ultimately be completed by a transition to the qualitatively different level of analysis represented by epistemology.[12] Epistemology assumes the reality of the de facto contents of subjective religious awareness that the psychology of religion has established. The epistemological investigation of mental phenomena then reflects upon the nature and scope of human knowledge in general in its efforts to affirm the truth of intrapsychic religious experience.

In the course of his inquiry into religion on the epistemological level, Troeltsch appealed primarily to the philosophical resources of critical idealism as he tried to establish the validity of subjective religious experience. For a period of almost a decade in the middle of his intellectual career, Troeltsch devoted considerable attention to the thought and writings of Immanuel Kant, striving to incorporate the diverse insights of Kantian philosophy within his own scientific enterprise. Troeltsch's own efforts to validate inner religious life, however, led him eventually to modify or extrapolate from the basic principles of Kantian epistemology in order to accomplish his desired goals. These efforts ultimately led to his postulating the concept of the religious a priori, by which the truth of personal religiosity may ostensibly be verified.[13]

Stated simply, the religious a priori designates a particular epistemic structure, or law of validity, which exists within human consciousness. Its primary function is to actuate, as well as to regulate and control, all mental experience classified as religious. This primordial form of consciousness, in Troeltsch's view, exists alongside all other fundamental laws of validity traditionally recognized by critical idealism. These include the logical or theoretical, the practical, and the aesthetic laws of consciousness. Each in its own way governs the range of experience which falls within its jurisdiction. In addition to assuming parallel functions within cognitive experience, however, all members of this group of discrete epistemic forms which constitute human consciousness share a status within mental reality as the autonomous, unconditioned, and universal dimension of human cognition which makes possible human knowledge in the first place. As necessary and intrinsic features of consciousness, these a priori structures reflect more than the arbitrary mental schemata of mere individuals. They also represent the universally valid categories of mental life which transcend and surpass all subjective experience. By applying the criterion of intersubjectivity uniformly to all types of consciousness, Troeltsch posits that the reality of the religious a priori guarantees the validity and truth of all specifically religious human experience, insofar as this category is a universal and necessary feature of human rationality in general. (Such assurances, however, remain limited to the experience of the subject and do not also extend to the actual existence of the religious object, towards which only an agnostic attitude is appropriate.) On the basis of the epistemological analysis endorsed and enhanced by Troeltsch, inner religious events are thereby recognized as something more than the capricious experience of individuals. They are in some way true, even as the issue of the objective reality of the transsubjective religious objects of belief remains an open question. Epistemology, in the final analysis, "cannot do more than indicate an a priori law of the formation of religious ideas existing in the nature of reason and standing in an organic relationship to the other a priori principles of reason. It can only undertake to deliver the proof for the necessity of the formation of religious ideas in reason, but not for the existence of the religious object itself. Epistemology can only achieve a binding validity for the contents of consciousness which are present . . . but it does not produce evidences of existence of each" (RSR 116).

The Turn to History

The first step in Troeltsch's outline for the scientific treatment of religion—designated above as the turn to the subject—represents his attempt to do justice to religion as a datum which manifests itself concretely in the inner life of religious individuals. Troeltsch's program here incorporates the different but related tasks of the psychological description of subjective religious events and the epistemological analysis of the cognitive structures which support them. The object of inquiry in both cases, however, is religion as it exists within human consciousness, apart from any spatial or temporal matrix. Intrapsychic religious experience in its primary forms is divorced from the particularity of religious traditions as they are rooted in specific geopolitical milieux. It is also lacking in any distinct historical reference to the shared occurrences which cohesively bind together through time members of a religious community. Yet, as Troeltsch insists so frequently in his writings, the range of empirical phenomena which may be identified as religious exceeds the self-imposed limits of interiority found at this initial moment in the scientific examination of religion. In order to accommodate religion in all its factuality, one must also include a turn to history within the program for the science of religion as its second branch. Only in this manner is it possible to address the extension of religion into exterior reality, as it is embodied in the various positive religions of human history and as it coalesces in tangible social or institutional forms within these traditions.[14]

If we may identify one of the fundamental directions of nineteenth-century religious thought as the turn to the subject, then such an orientation was accompanied by a corresponding historical turn. While the leading critical thinkers of this century sought to demonstrate how religiosity is localized in human consciousness, many of them also tried to show that history is equally the realm of religious experience. In so doing, they were both inspired by the receptivity of Romanticism toward other religions as part of the historico-cultural wealth of humanity, and informed by the explosion of sheer information uncovered or recovered by the newly sophisticated historical sciences. The burgeoning discipline known alternatively as the history of religions or comparative religion gradually assumed a position of prominence within the emerging field of religious studies. When conjoined with apologetic efforts to establish the superiority of Christianity (by such thinkers as Schleiermacher, Hegel, and Ritschl), the data of the history of religion provided crucial insights into the relationship between Christianity and non-Christian religions. These insights then served as the basis for theological reflection on the truth of Christianity compared to other world religions. Concomitantly, the awareness of the historicity of all elements of human culture illuminated various aspects of the Christian religion itself. The immediate result was the rise of various scholarly enterprises which presupposed the temporal character of Christian life. These included, for example, a historically minded Biblical studies, church history, and the history of dogma. Thus, recognizing its dramatic impact upon the religious thought of the preceding century, Troeltsch readily incorporated the turn to history as the second moment within his own framework for the scientific investigation of religion.

What is the agenda of "the second great principal problem of the science of religion, the problem of the history of religion" (SR 72)? In "Die Selbständigkeit der Religion," Troeltsch concisely states its fundamental purpose. The primary task of the history of religions is to "seek law and coherence in the historical particulars of religion and the basis for a standard of value for the critical evaluation of these particulars" (SR 370). This enterprise must not be confused with historical science per se, which merely delineates the most salient empirical features of the religions of humankind. The history of religions is to be taken

> not in the sense of the investigation of [historical] detail, but rather in the sense of a critical understanding of the entire process of development. It concerns only the question of the understanding and evaluation of the history of religion. The descriptive and evolving history of particular religions, a nascent and still quite fragmentary science, and one rendered possible only by means of the philological and ethnological research of our century, is presupposed for this [critical task], as also for the earlier inquiry [into the psychology of religion]. [SR 72]

Thus, while assuming the results of traditional historiography, the history of religions moves decisively beyond the task of mere description to the more philosophical assignment of critical evaluation.[15] The latter task is necessitated by the extraordinary variety of religious traditions which are found within history. It is accomplished only by the systematic assessment of these traditions in terms of a clearly defined standard or criterion by which their relative validity may be measured.

In performing this task, Troeltsch acknowledged the valuable philosophical and theological resources made available by his nineteenth-century predecessors. These included, in particular, the Hegelian paradigm of history discussed in detail in chapter 2. Indeed, according to Troeltsch, the "finest solution of this task [of the philosophy of the history of religion] so far lies in the teaching of Hegel" (RSR 117). Nevertheless, despite its preeminence, the Hegelian response to the problem at hand, in Troeltsch's eyes, had its questionable features. Troeltsch maintained that Hegel correctly identified the goal to which the philosophy of the history of religions must aspire, but asserted that it "must be reached by other logical and methodological paths" (RSR 117).

To recapitulate, the centerpiece of Hegel's efforts to discern law and coherence within the religious history of humanity, and so to assess the various historical religions, is the concept of evolutionary development, grounded upon an explicitly metaphysical interpretation of history. According to Hegel, the interconnection among the variety of historical religions is visible by regarding history as a unilinear developmental process permeated by the divine Reason. The Absolute pervades world history in order gradually to attain its desired goal of self-knowledge or self-consciousness. This telos of history, so defined, in turn provides the law or norm by which each of the major moments of religious history may be evaluated. More specifically, the religious traditions are assessed and graded in terms of the relative degree to which they embody the progressive advance of the World Spirit toward its own final goal. Thus, each of the major world religions corresponds to an increasingly more adequate stage of divine self-knowledge and is accordingly assigned an appropriate position along this developmental ladder. This process, in Hegel's view, inexorably culminates with Spirit's achievement of complete and perfect self-awareness through the medium of one particular historical religion—namely, Christianity (or the absolute religion). In this way, Hegel satisfies the primary requirement of the philosophy of the history of religions.

In light of Hegel's solution to the central problem of the history of religions, what degree of congruence exists between the Hegelian paradigm and Troeltsch's own proposed response? First, and most importantly, for Troeltsch as for Hegel, is the notion of development. This key conceptual tool provides the theoretical underpinning for their respective endeavors to address this issue. In Troeltsch's view, the attempt to comprehend the inner unity of history that underlies the immense variety of its positive religious formations requires that one posit "a teleological law of development" (RSR 117). By understanding history as a developmental process directed toward a specific goal, the various historical forms of religions may be brought together and arranged in a coherent manner. The linkage among the world religions is established by locating them as part of a sequence of temporally contiguous, advancing stages. A rational justification is thus given for seeing the continuity and interrelationships among the particular religions of world history and for recognizing the relative validity of each. For this reason, Troeltsch enthusiastically affirms that the notion of progressive development represents "the final and most important concept of all philosophy of history" (RSR 117).

In so doing, moreover, Troeltsch self-consciously acknowledges his debt to Hegel and the latter's philosophical disciples, by whom he was persuaded of the value of this category for understanding the lawful dynamics of world history. As part of a lengthy footnoote in "Geschichte und Metaphysik," Troeltsch writes, "I was [early on] referred to the concept of development, which had then been taught by Hegel and the Hegelians."[16] According to Troeltsch, it is only necessary to follow those successors of Hegel who have liberated the notion of development from "the special Hegelian theory of the dialectic of the Absolute" (SR 177). Abstracting the development of a determinate area of life from "the universal ontological framework of the self-movement of the Absolute Concept, dialectically spinning forth nature and history from itself" (SR 177), thereby provides, in Troeltsch's view, a necessary corrective to Hegel's philosophy of history. Temporally delimited areas of human life, including especially the realm of religious history, may be examined. The inner connection to be found there may be discerned independently of the dialectical movement of the Absolute. Troeltsch fully endorsed this reinterpretation of Hegel's concept of development.

Troeltsch thus rejected a rigid interpretation of development in terms of its strict relationship to the dialectic of the Absolute. He nevertheless shared Hegel's patently metaphysical presuppositions regarding world history. Like Hegel, Troeltsch believed that there is something more to history than the human elements which constitute the essence of historical movement. For both thinkers, the source of history's vitality is the self-movement of the divine Reason itself. History is best understood as a process of divine self-expression. As God's progressive self-revelation, the particular historical formations of religion are grounded in an absolute sphere of reality, so ensuring their truth. The development of religion must be understood

> as the self-communication of the divine Spirit, and we must trust that in this self-communication the truth of religion progressively reveals itself. Hegel's merit is to have referred to this necessity of an objective divine correlate to the merely subjective course of history. Such is in fact absolutely necessary, if one is certainly to be able to believe in the truth of religion in general. . . . Hegel's mistake was only that he believed that he could construct this self-communication of God out of the essence of the Absolute, as he had defined it. With that the history of religion dissolved in an intellectualistic dialectic of the concept. [SR 80–81]

With Hegel, then, Troeltsch, could speak of the "divine humanity of the history of religions" (SR 83), whereby the finite and Infinite are intimately intertwined in our religious history, rather than radically separated from one another. For Troeltsch, such a vision of the "interpenetration of divine and human effects" (SR 83) in history is "thoroughly a matter of faith" (SR 79) and so is "inaccessible to science" (SR 83). But his conviction still holds "that the reason which holds sway in the human spirit also governs generally in the world, and here, as there, includes an impulse to the unfolding and exposition of its ultimate meaning and deepest contents. . . . All human history on the whole is not merely a succession of human subjectivities, but rather a cooperative venture of human spirits with the divine ground of the world" (SR 79).

Nevertheless, despite his willingness to appropriate certain essential features of Hegel's thought, Troeltsch's implementation of the essential task of the philosophy of the history of religions departs significantly from the Hegelian paradigm as well. They agreed that history is best construed as a developmental process, pervaded by the divine Reason, in terms of which lawful interconnections among historical phenomena may be established. This consensus, however, is qualified by their disagreement regarding the proper method of grading and ranking the positive religions which manifest themselves within human history. More specifically, the central difference between Troeltsch and Hegel concerns the status and origin of the criterion of evaluation used to assess the historical varieties of religion in the course of their development. As we have seen, Troeltsch commended Hegel's intention successfully to resolve the basic problematic of the philosophy of the history of religions. But Troeltsch vigorously objected to the means which Hegel used to determine the normative standard employed to appraise religious history. According to Troeltsch, authentic historical thinking requires that any such criterion be arrived at inductively by the simple exposure of investigators to the vital forces of history itself. As they immerse themselves within the stream of history, the most relevant standard of evaluation will, in effect, rise up and overwhelm them by virtue of its own intrinsic and self-evident superiority.

> There is not any ready-made standard, according to which one could evaluate the development, progress and goal [of history]. The standard grows in and with history itself, in that the higher manifestation carries in itself the certainty of its greater power and depth. . . . In the history of religions nothing else remains than to entrust oneself to the actual procession of ideas and there to seek the goal where it manifests itself through the power of facts, through the superiority over [all] preliminary stages, the inner power of the capacity for inspiration, and through the breadth of its capacity for adaptation. [SR 78]

The negative implications of this passage for assessing the viability of the Hegelian paradigm should be obvious. Despite Hegel's good intentions, according to Troeltsch, his method of deriving the criterion of evaluation is fundamentally misguided. As we have seen, Hegel proposed a priori to deduce from the essence of God itself the norm by which to assay the history of religions, rather than a posteriori to infer its nature from history, as recommended by Troeltsch. The Hegelian standard of judgment thus lacks any real rootedness in history. It is instead deductively derived by way of purely philosophical considerations, stemming from his concept of the Absolute. In Troeltsch's eyes, then, Hegel's solution to the primary task of the history of religions represents a crude violation of real history itself, and so must be adjudged a failure. Despite their shared purpose in this endeavor, the realities of historical life, in Troeltsch's view, demand a dismissal of the methodological path taken by his predecessor. "I need not further pursue, how far this resigned surrender to reality relinquishes the omniscience of Hegel, who possessed in the dialectically self-moving Concept the key to all the mysteries of the world and accordingly . . . recognized and construed only the historically self-explicating Concept of absolute Spirit, comprehending itself in its concrete fullness in Christianity" (SR 93–94).

Notwithstanding these procedural differences, however, Troeltsch is substantially in accord with Hegel's conclusions regarding the summit of our religious history. In "Die Selbständigkeit der Religion," Troeltsch briefly reviews this history, in order to facilitate "an evaluation of religious development" (SR 175). His survey tracks four primary religious concepts—God, world, the soul, and redemption—in order to discern its direction and developmental goal. On the basis of its understanding of each of these foundational concepts, Troeltsch concluded that Christianity alone among the great world religions embodies the standard by which the entire history of religion may most appropriately be evaluated. As such, it represents the highest product of the religious idea.

> The inner dialectic of the religious idea points in the direction of the perfectly individual and thus universalistic religion of redemption, which can only be so, because it is perfectly spiritualized and moralized. The facts show that, of all religions, those moving in this direction are those alone which advance, and those pursuing it most intensely are the most vital and victorious and are bound to the highest cultures. With this is given the standard of evaluation which we seek. . . . Even with the most rigorous scientific objectivity, there can be no doubt about it. It is as clear as day that Christianity is the deepest, the most powerful and the richest development of the religious idea. [SR 200]

Contra Hegel, Troeltsch rejects the notion that any religion (including Christianity) can claim absolute status in the sense that this term is employed within the Hegelian paradigm. Yet Troeltsch shares with Hegel the conclusion that Christianity somehow occupies a privileged place among the world religions—indeed, that it represents the culmination of the development thus far of the history of religions. Even in the absence of direct, scientifically verifiable proof of its special status, Troeltsch can assert that the Christian religion is qualitatively different from all other religions. "The difference between Christianity and other religions is not one of 'more or less.' It is a difference in principle over against all others" (SR 204). For both Troeltsch and Hegel, then, there is substantive agreement that the Christian religion represents the zenith of the history of religion. This is a position which Troeltsch will retain, albeit with more reservations, in *Die Absolutheit des Christentums*.

The Influence of Hegel in Troeltsch's Early Writings

The preceding discussion of Troeltsch's proposed implementation of the basic task of the history of religion concludes my exposition of his science of religion in particular, and, in general, his efforts to establish the integrity and autonomy of religion. Such efforts, as we have seen, were initiated in the face of the modern spiritual crisis which engulfed both Christianity and all generic expressions of religious life. The final outcome of his scientific investigation into religion discloses that, for Troeltsch, religion is an independent sphere of human reality, both psychical and historical, and is generated and regulated by its own intrinsic laws. "Religion is a uniform phenomenon, that moves about in connection with the entire sphere of spiritual life, but does so according to its own laws. It affirms a relative independence in the face of all other areas of life. The truth of its own formations must be sought out from within religion itself, and it only discloses and receives its total meaning and content in its historical movement and particularity" (SR 369–70).

Of greater significance for this project, my analysis of these issues has led to an explicit consideration of Troeltsch's relationship to the Hegelian paradigm during the first major phase of Troeltsch's intellectual career. Based on this analysis, I argue that Troeltsch's attitude toward Hegel, within the specific context in which he sought out the contributions and insights of his predecessor, reflects a studied ambivalence. Such mixed feelings appear to resemble those felt by other thinkers who have grappled with the Hegelian legacy. "If I have linked myself with Hegel and have even drawn near to the Hegelian philosophers of religion, I have thereby expressly explained that this has occurred not for the sake of Hegel's metaphysics of the Absolute. Rather, I have done so for the sake of that force of the concept of development, which no one has analyzed as sharply and as clearly as he has done, and which has become a possession of the common good, even of those who hold him to be a 'master' who has been completely overcome."[17]

On the one hand, the positive influence of Hegel on Troeltsch's own efforts to address the methodological issues raised by his formulation of the task of the science of religion is transparent. Hegel's influence may be traced in Troeltsch's approval of the notion of historical development; his willing appeal to a metaphysical interpretation of history as the ultimate means by which the religious values of human experience may be validated and affirmed; and his conclusion that Christianity in some way represents the final goal of the development of the religious history of humanity. On the other hand, it is equally apparent that even at the outset of his career, Troeltsch distanced himself from Hegel, in the name of real history, concerning the precise path to be taken in determining the standard by which the development of religious history should be assessed. Hegel reached his conclusion deductively. He obtained his standard of measurement from the nature and goal of the divine Reason rather than from material located within the historical process itself. Troeltsch reached his verdict inductively, from within history, by abstracting the criterion of assessment from the historical data themselves.

Even in the initial writings of Troeltsch considered in this chapter, then, we can ascertain a judicious reaction by Troeltsch to the Hegelian paradigm that supports the central thesis of this essay. My elucidation of Troeltsch's critical relation to Hegel thus far reveals elements of both continuity and discontinuity with the Hegelian legacy. In both subtle and obvious ways, this general pattern, as well as many of the same substantive issues examined above, reemerges in subsequent phases of his intellectual career where the ghost of Hegel lurks in the background of Troeltsch's thought.

Historical Relativism and the Crisis of Religious Values: Troeltsch's Critique of Hegel in *Die Absolutheit des Christentums*

Christianity and the Problem of "Absoluteness"

"It may be taken for granted," Troeltsch writes at the outset of his transitional lecture/essay of 1902,[1] "that the modern world, in the great and dominating forms it has assumed since the eighteenth century, represents a unique type of culture" (AC 45). Notwithstanding the diversity of intellectual movements discussed in chapter 3, Troeltsch insists that its trademark feature was the relatively recent rise to prominence of "an unreservedly historical view of human affairs" (AC 45). Inspired by Enlightenment canons of autonomy and rationality and a questioning temper of mind, and influenced by concurrent philosophical movements of a humanistic bent, the study of history gradually emerged as a viable mode of critical inquiry into the collective life of humankind (past and present), on a par with both the natural and social sciences.[2]

The modern idea of history was novel both in its methodological presuppositions and in its scholarly techniques. In Troeltsch's opinion, however, it was no less revolutionary in its profound influence upon our thinking about the values and norms upon which our cultural and religious life is based. The growth of knowledge generated by historical reflection upon both the present and the past produced an indelible impression of the seemingly endless pluralism of historical life. Moreover, the historical investigation of all components of human culture inevitably followed the withdrawal of immunity against such inquiry from every cultural system and religious tradition. This disclosed the fundamental historicity of all such movements, as their rootedness in a particular temporal environment was increasingly recognized. Consequently, the heretofore sacrosanct truth-claims of any given system of cultural or religious values began to lose their inviolability as that system's ideals and standards were acknowledged as relative both to the analogous truth-claims of all other cultures and religions and to the particular historical milieu from which they emerged. The primary result of the rise of Western historical consciousness was that "the original naïve certainty held by every existing type of culture and value system regarding the obviousness of its own validity has been shaken. Each culture, each value system, is treated as one object of historical investigation among others" (AC 46). Stated more simply, the problem of absoluteness had presented itself, as previously indubitable normative standards were subjected to the challenge of history. Confronted by the crisis of historical relativism, the modern religious person was impelled to answer "the momentous and radical question of our intellectual, or at least of our religious situation. This question is: How can we pass beyond the diversity with which history presents us to norms for our faith and for our judgments about life?" (AC 61).

Despite the originally unreflective self-assurance of its proponents regarding its normative truth, Christianity, like all other religions, eventually became vulnerable to the crisis posed by modern historical thinking.[3] Rather than retreat or surrender before it, however, various Christian theologians formulated apologetic strategies that argued for the absoluteness of Christian truth-claims as compared to those of other religious traditions, including the supernatural theory of orthodoxy and the evolutionary theory of modern theology. These theories are, in Troeltsch's view, "the only ones that require serious consideration in an inquiry concerning the 'absoluteness' of Christianity" (AC 56). Both theories are informed by the same fundamental motive and goal—namely, "to establish the normative value of Christian thought" (AC 51). Moreover, "both the evolutionary and the orthodox schools of thought desire to attain this normative value by placing Christianity, as a matter of principle, in a unique position. They are not content with a de facto supremacy and ultimacy but want to make it into the sole truth to which everything else stands opposed in accordance with the requirements of theory" (AC 51). Nevertheless, despite this shared intention, the orthodox and evolutionary theories differ dramatically as to the specific means which each employs to achieve its desired end. In the opening pages of *Die Absolutheit des Christentums*, Troeltsch examines and appraises each apologetic strategy in turn.

The Supernatural Apologetic Theory

According to Troeltsch, the apologetic strategy of orthodoxy guaranteed the absoluteness of Christianity by the central notion of exclusive supernatural revelation, in the form of divine miracles, upon which it is based. From its perspective, a radical dichotomy exists between Christianity and everything outside Christianity taken as a whole. The latter in its entirety is seen as nothing more than an undifferentiated sphere of sin-induced fallacy grounded merely on human activity. The former, in contrast, is regarded as nothing less than the sole locus of "truth that is absolutely certain" (AC 47) in the world. Such absolutist truth-claims on the part of the Christian religion are legitimated, according to its orthodox apologists, by the efficacy of a special divine causality. This causality is operative at decisive moments throughout the continuing history of Christianity. By its very nature, it "in principle lies beyond all human fallibility and impotence" (AC 52). Originally founded by the archetypal, once-for-all external miracle of the Incarnation (as well as other contemporaneous salvific acts to which the Bible attests), the Christian faith is continually authenticated by the inner psychological miracle of conversion and spiritual renewal within the hearts of believers that transcends all natural powers. It thereby qualifies as a thoroughly unique phenomenon in human history, one that "stands within history but does not derive from history" (AC 47). By tracing its origin and later development directly to the miraculous intervention of God, and by positing that such miraculous activity functions exclusively in the arena of Christian faith, members of this theological school thus claim to have established the supernatural status of the Christian religion. In this way do they claim as well to have validated the absolute quality of its beliefs and norms.

As Troeltsch notes further, however, the defects of the supernatural apologetic are painfully obvious to any critic with the least amount of historical sophistication. Hence, its survival in the modern world is at best a dubious prospect. For various reasons, "the modern idea of history . . . has had a radically dissolving effect on this apologetic structure of thought" (AC 47–48). First of all, the sheer awareness of the salient features of other religious traditions, brought about by critical historical investigation, poses an acute problem for its claim that Christianity is historically unique. The resultant recognition of the fundamental similarity between Christianity and other religions in all phases of religious life (including such apparently widespread phenomena as miracles) can only undermine the notion that the Christian religion is qualitatively different from its extra-Christian counterparts. Christian apologists may retain this notion, therefore, only by risking the blatant logical inconsistency that must accompany the denial of the corresponding claims of other religions. Without a theory of exclusive miraculous causation, however, one of the essential grounds for maintaining the singular truth of Christianity is thereby forsaken.

> The apologetic wall of division, the wall of external and internal miracle, has slowly been broken down by this idea of history, for no matter what one may otherwise think about miracles, it is impossible for historical thought to believe the Christian miracles but deny the non-Christian. . . . With this, however, there no longer exists any means by which one may isolate Christianity from the rest of history and then, on the basis of this isolation and its formal signs, define it as an absolute norm. [AC 48]

Second, and more important, Troeltsch suggests that, in light of modern historical thinking, any apologetic theory based on miracle (Christian or otherwise) is susceptible to potentially devastating criticism. In *Die Absolutheit des Christentums,* Troeltsch states his conclusions rather tersely. However, in "Ueber historische und dogmatische Methode in der Theologie," Troeltsch provides the methodological basis for his argument in principle against the notion of a special divine or miraculous causality allegedly efficacious in any given religious tradition. In this essay, Troeltsch identifies the three fundamental principles of the historical method as the practice of historical criticism, the principle of analogy, and the postulation of the interconnection of all occurrences in human history. When taken together, these three interrelated canons of historiography, in his view, necessarily eliminate the possibility that the historical process may be disrupted by the supernatural, miraculous events upon which the orthodox apologetic theory relies.

Troeltsch assumes that all historical events are essentially similar to each other, as the principle of analogy contends. If so, then the radically unique occurrences that "defy the homogeneity of history"

(AC 60), to which orthodoxy appeals for its dogmatic assertions regarding the absoluteness of Christianity, must be judged to be highly improbable, if not, indeed, impossible. They lack any features resembling phenomena with which historians are familiar. Students of history, therefore, can only affirm the relative unlikelihood that the reputed historical miracles of the Christian tradition ever occurred. Moreover, the supernatural apologetic differentiates between the sacred events of Christianity and profane history. The former derive "directly from God"; the latter is a "sphere of sin and error" with "its merely human and humanly conditioned truths" (AC 47). The Christian religion is thereby isolated from the rest of history. On this basis, its orthodox apologists claim for it absolute normativeness divorced from any real consideration of alternative religious traditions. From the historical point of view, however, all events are inextricably linked together along an all-inclusive continuum of mutually conditioning antecedent and subsequent occurrences. As a result, any extreme polarization between sacred and profane history is rendered meaningless. Accordingly, historical criticism again leads to an attitude of disbelief concerning the intrusion of occurrences from beyond, or outside of, this nexus. For Troeltsch, then, orthodox Christian faith, with its dependence upon the absolute uniqueness of certain ostensibly factual events, defies the fundamental presuppositions upon which modern historical thought is grounded. For this reason, the supernatural apologetic strategy inevitably "gasps for breath the more it breathes the air of the modern understanding of history" (AC 60).[4]

In sum, Troeltsch's appraisal of the traditional apologetic strategy of orthodox theology leads him inescapably to conclude that its fundamental maxims have been thoroughly subverted by the critical historical approach. The application of a historical critique to this theological theory is what "ultimately justifies a skeptical outlook that opposes the various means by which Christianity has been isolated from other human history—means that have been used . . . to demonstrate the normative truth of Christianity solely out of its own resources without a single glance at other history" (AC 48–49). However, when Troeltsch considers the second major apologetic proof of the absoluteness of the Christian religion—the evolutionary theory of modern theology—he is noticeably more enthusiastic. Disdaining the complete separation of Christianity from the rest of history recommended by the orthodox apologist, advocates of the evolutionary apologetic theory chose instead to incorporate the Christian religion within the larger context of the entire history of religions. In so doing, they sought to secure a favored position for Christianity in relation to other religious traditions. "Its starting-point was the concept of a total history of mankind, with history taken as a dynamic principle in its own right" (AC 49). "Thus," as Troeltsch writes, "the older apologetic speculation, which opposed history, has been replaced by a new one that is on the side of history" (AC 50). For this reason, despite his keen appreciation of its striking deficiencies, Troeltsch states with satisfaction that "the idealistic-evolutionary theory" is "the only one that calls for serious critical consideration" in light of the modern idea of history (AC 60).

The Evolutionary Apologetic Theory

Engendered primarily by Hegel[5] (and discussed in greater detail in chapter 2), the evolutionary apologetic, as its name suggests, is based primarily upon the concept of evolutionary development. From its perspective, the overall structure of the history of humanity (especially its religious history) is construed as an ascending series. Within this series, "the ideal of religious truth was thought of as moving forward in gradual stages" (AC 49) corresponding to the various world-historical religions. According to this scheme, the later (or higher) stages of history have emerged directly from earlier (or lower) ones. The latter are the necessary forerunners of the former, and all stages are located along a single path of unilinear progression. Moreover, in its Hegelian form (which Troeltsch designates as "speculative evolutionism" [AC 73]), this entire developmental process is seen as grounded in, and generated by, a singular germinative nucleus. Eternal, absolute, and divine in nature, this universal causal principle creates world history out of the essence of its own being by unfolding or positing itself in and as the world of historical reality. It is "a uniform, homogeneous, law-structured, and self-actuating power that brings forth individual instances of itself" (AC 66). This stands in striking contrast to the orthodox apologetic, for which the divine is a supernatural phenomenon which must cleave miraculously through natural processes in its various acts of self-revelation. The apologetic theory of modern theology regards the world as the medium in and through which this universal principle manifests itself. The Absolute is here conceived primarily as immanent within the world, "unfolding its inner life-content in gradual movement through the [natural and historical] structures of causality," rather than as an entity which is qualitatively different from this "causal context" (AC 53).

As Troeltsch notes further, the process of evolutionary development within this conceptual framework is interpreted in teleological (as well as causal) terms. World history as a whole is seen as a process evolving in a definite sequence toward an ultimate telos intrinsic to the divine principle itself. This telos is the self-realization or self-actualization of this principle. According to Troeltsch, causality and finality are conjoined in the divine principle. It was envisioned as one "that bore within itself the law of its movement from lower, obscure, and embryonic beginnings to complete, clear, and conscious maturity—a universal principle represented as a normative power actualizing itself by degrees in the course of history" (AC 66). Moreover, this telos, abstracted from the concept of the universal principle itself, serves as the criterion by which the different stages of world history may be discerned and evaluated. Because of its normative function, the application of this ideal to the various world religions of history makes it possible to appraise their value along the scale of evolutionary development, according to the degree to which they approach or approximate the goal of the divine in history.

Finally, this apologetic theory maintained that this goal has already been reached at one definite point in world history. The divine Idea must first "gradually reveal its content and essence within the total meaning and context of human reality and in conjunction with man's unfolding of the depths of his own consciousness. But the Idea must also attain the perfect goal, the absolute principle, in which all that was previously revealed as circumscribed, in process, and preliminary finds its ultimate conclusion" (AC 54). Though implicit in all phases of the historical process, the divine is regarded as having explicitly reached its ultimate goal of absolute self-realization in the particular historical phenomenon of the Christian religion. Accordingly, Christianity represents the apex of history. Hence, it is designated as the "absolute religion in antithesis to mediated and veiled expressions of this principle" (AC 49). "In Christianity this universally latent essence, everywhere else limited by its media, has appeared in untrammeled and exhaustive perfection" (AC 49).[6] In sum, then, the concept of evolutionary development, the notion of a universal principle operative both causally and teleologically in world history, and the idea of the absolute realization of this divine principle within history in historical Christianity, together constitute the three discrete but correlative doctrines upon which the apologetic strategy of modern theology has been constructed.

The evolutionary theory, when employed by Christian theologians, proved exceedingly useful in the apologetic quest to establish Christianity's supremacy. Like that of orthodoxy, this strategy ultimately affirms the absoluteness of Christianity on the basis of the historical singularity of the Christian religion. On its terms, however, this uniqueness does not finally derive from the isolation of Christianity from the larger context of world history. Its status as the absolute religion is not acquired at the expense of all other history. Rather, it is due precisely to its special position within the framework of humanity's total history that the apologetic theory of orthodoxy rejects. For the modern apologist, the remainder of human history is also in its own way the realm of religious truth, albeit of a partial or relative nature. This is so insofar as all historical religions are grounded in the same eternal, universal principle which runs throughout world history as its ultimate source and final goal. "All religion is . . . truth from God, each religion corresponds to some stage in a universal process of spiritual development" (AC 54). By the same token, "there must also be a highest, ultimate stage that demonstrates itself to be so through its fulfillment of the evolutionary law intrinsic to the universal principle that is the basis of all things" (AC 54). Only as the culmination of the historical process and as the complete and exhaustive realization of the Idea in history that is elsewhere only tacit, is Christianity regarded as possessing truth that is absolutely normative. In the final analysis, the believing observer of the religious history of humankind must only discern the hierarchical structure of interrelationships which exists among world religions. In this way, both the relative validity of all non-Christian religions and the absolute truth of Christianity may be acknowledged.

> The man of faith sees this inner [universal] principle evolving everywhere according to strict laws that follow from the nature of divine activity. On the basis of these laws of evolutionary development, he recognizes in devout admiration the inevitable preeminence of the summit on which he stands. From this summit he commands a view over all the divine powers of earthly history and reverently foresees the ultimate completion of all the purposes and powers at work in this history. From this perspective, tangled reality becomes crystal clear and what seemed to be chaos is transformed into a wondrous realm of transparently obvious consequences. A kind of religious geology teaches such a man to understand all lands and provinces in this realm as preliminary stages to the summit they all help to form, the summit that exists not in isolation from all else but simply as the crown of the whole. [AC 54].

I have noted that Troeltsch's sympathies rest with the Hegelian theory of the absoluteness of Christianity, alienated and embarrassed as he and other like-minded persons are by the contra-historical features of the orthodox theory. Nevertheless, Troeltsch's decided preference for the evolutionary apologetic of modern theology cannot disguise his own scepticism regarding its ability to serve as an altogether "tenable alternative to the doctrine of exclusive supernatural revelation" (AC 61). Unfortunately, the evolutionary theory of modern theology, "when viewed from the perspective of the modern idea of history, stands in utter contradiction to real events" (AC 73). Thus, in the name of real history, Troeltsch launches a critique of the evolutionary apologetic on multiple fronts. He itemizes the various "irrefutable objections" (AC 66) which may be brought against it, in anticipation of his own solution to the problem of historical relativism. In the last analysis, Troeltsch's conclusions regarding the modern apologetic theory associated with the Hegelian paradigm, despite its apparent superiority over the supernatural model, are "essentially negative" (AC 61). For Troeltsch, the evolutionary apologetic is not a totally viable option even on its own terms. It must be replaced by a more satisfactory theoretical approach to the problem at hand.

In the course of his polemic against the apologetic theory of modern theology, Troeltsch identifies several liabilities associated with its central concept of evolutionary development. These, he feels, illustrate the deficiencies of this theory as a whole. As we saw in chapter 3, Troeltsch is by no means unequivocally critical of this notion. Indeed, he is appreciative of its obvious utility for understanding the continuity and growth characteristic of the dynamic element of history.

> In and of itself this concept is one of the most reliable working tools there is, and it is one of the fundamental presuppositions of the scientific study of history. It has proved its worth beyond all shadow of doubt and corresponds to all knowable processes in the sense that everywhere, whether in large matters or small, elemental points of departure have to be assumed, on the basis of which the more complex life of matter and spirit arises through a combination of resistance and assimilation. It is equally certain that all the great creative urges, ideas, and animating powers that break forth in this evolutionary process first appeared in primitive embryonic forms and disclosed their true content only in accommodation and antithesis, in growing depth and unfolding of implications, in reflection and struggle that lasted through many generations. To an outlook that faces the past, the forces that have burst forth in this way must accordingly appear as life-principles or creative energies that develop in accordance with their own inner logic. [AC 72–73]

Despite recognizing the genuine value of this concept for the purpose of historical analysis, however, Troeltsch in *Die Absolutheit des Christentums* harshly criticizes its application by the apologetic theory that has appropriated it. First, merely on the level of empirical historical investigation, the student of history cannot discern within the history of religions the progressive ascent or unilinear development postulated by the Hegelian paradigm. According to Troeltsch, the more knowledge one attains regarding humanity's religious history (especially the religions of the Oriental world), the less confidently one may talk about higher and lower stages in the history of the religious consciousness. Indeed, rather than identifying an evolutionary development of the world religions along a single channel, the historically minded student of religion is apt to regard the diverse religious traditions that have emerged in human history as separate but equal phenomena. They are not, to be sure, entities which have appeared in total isolation from other religions. This would violate Troeltsch's own principles of historical thinking. Neither, however, may they arbitrarily be assigned a specific rung on the alleged evolutionary ladder of world history.

> The modern study of history gives no indication whatever of any graded progression such as this theory might lead us to expect. History manifests no gradual ascent to higher orientations as far as the vast majority of mankind is concerned. Only at special points do higher orientations burst forth, and then in a great, soaring development of their uniquely individual content. By no means, however, are the great religions that burst forth in this way related to each other in a stage-by-stage causal process. They stand, rather, in a parallel relationship. The only path to an understanding of their relationship in terms of value is toil and inner moral struggle, not schemes of progressive development like those that are always being constructed. Since it is no longer merely the history of religion in the Near East and in the cultures around the Mediterranean but also the world of the East Asian religions that stands before our eyes, we can no longer deceive ourselves about this matter. [AC 69–70]

Troeltsch's more serious reservations about the concept of evolutionary development, however, concern certain theoretical difficulties which arise especially from its linkage to the notion of universal causality, a notion for which he has little regard. Troeltsch writes in the foreword to the first edition of *Die Absolutheit* that "I contest the universal applicability of the causal view, in the sense of a closed system of necessary causes and effects, as far as historical phenomena and the entire compass of human events are concerned" (AC 31). Unfortunately for his readers, however, Troeltsch is not forthcoming in indicating precisely how his antipathy toward monocausal theories of history in general may be applied in particular to the Hegelian model of history. Rather, in *Die Absolutheit des Christentums*

Troeltsch couches his response to such theories primarily in terms of a rejection of all so-called naturalistic modes of historical explanation. Such explanatory models attempt to understand the data and processes of history in terms drawn from the worldview of the natural sciences.

According to Troeltsch, the main premise of any naturalistic theory of historical explanation is that all historical phenomena are the direct products of a set of preexistent variables drawn from the natural realm of existence (for example, biological needs, physical perceptions and sensations, psychological drives, etc.). From this perspective, the former ostensibly emerge from, or are caused by, the latter. Such causation is governed by various natural and social-scientific laws which regulate the psycho-physical processes of human life. The fatal flaw of this explanatory model, however, is the irremediable violence which it does to the uniqueness and individuality endemic to all historical phenomena. These are characteristics which Troeltsch, following the lead of the neo-Kantian philosophers among his contemporaries, identifies as definitive of entities belonging to the historical realm.[7] From the point of view of the naturalistic mode of explanation, all historical objects ultimately may be derived from, and, hence, essentially reduced to, the common denominator of the natural realm. Accordingly, nothing that is truly original or unique can emerge in human existence. All historical phenomena are construed merely as rearrangements or rearticulations of a pre-given set of natural principles. "Here . . . there is nothing really *new* and hence no transcending of the pure givenness of nature with its endless interplay of already existent forces" (AC 86).

In decided contrast to this theoretical perspective, Troeltsch affirms an alternative position. He acknowledges the formative role which the natural structures and conditions of life play in history, but he unequivocally renounces the view that they are the sole determinative factors in the historical world. As Troeltsch notes, the physical infrastructure of existence undeniably serves as the fundamental matrix out of which all manifestations of human life originate, thereby shaping and conditioning them (at least in part). However, above and beyond this naturalistic base, Troeltsch posits the reality of a second dimension of human existence. It coexists beside this natural foundation, but it functions as an independent sphere of life.

From the angle of vision afforded by the modern understanding of history there always exists an indissoluble distinction between the perceptions, thoughts, and desires that
accompany man as a physical entity in the realm of nature
and the higher, creative element in man that intervenes and
opposes them. This higher, creative element, for all its involvement in perceptions, thoughts, and desires of this kind,
leads its own autonomous life and can therefore under no
circumstances be classified with them under the concept of
a single, all-embracing causal principle. The modern understanding of history sees an encounter between opposed
forces wherever it looks, and it has only muddied the waters
of historical understanding when it has incorporated monistic theories into its work. [AC 64]

More important, this latter dimension of human life—at once
higher and deeper than the sphere of natural reality—serves as the
true locus and creative wellspring of all the intellectual, cultural, and
religious products of the human spirit which are associated with historical existence. Such effluvia, while susceptible to analysis and
description according to their own inner logic, ultimately emerge
spontaneously and, indeed, somewhat mysteriously from this particular source. Thus, they are neither directly reducible to a specific
prior cause nor explainable as a totally necessary departure from an
elemental matrix. Rather, they are best understood as highly original
creations. From the perspective of the model of historical analysis
proffered by Troeltsch, then, the fundamental uniqueness and individuality of all historical phenomena are preserved and maintained,
rather than jeopardized. Despite the necessary commingling of natural and spiritual forces in life, the latter cannot be reduced to, or
subsumed under, the former. They exist instead as the disparate
products of a self-standing realm of human life.

Troeltsch's critique of the notion of causality found in the naturalistic mode of historical explanation in turn sheds light on his dissat-
isfaction with the evolutionary apologetic strategy. This theory, like
the naturalistic model, explains the appearance of historical phenomena in terms of a singular source. It depicts that point of origin,
however, as a metaphysical principle, rather than a set of physical or
natural variables. But Troeltsch objects to any account of the total
life of humanity as a direct product of one (or several) ontologically

prior principles, however they may be construed. Such accounts by necessity reduce the higher creations of humankind found in the historical realm to epiphenomenal status, to be regarded as instances or derivatives of ostensibly more real forces of life. Thus, the postulate of the Hegelian paradigm that a single universal principle is operative in world history as the essential cause of all historical entities is, in its own way, as problematic as the naturalistic model of historical explanation. In defense of history against all such monistic interpretations, it must ultimately be rejected with equal force. "The modern idea of history knows no universal principle on the basis of which the content and sequence of events might be deduced. It knows only concrete, individual phenomena, always conditioned by their context and yet, at bottom, underivable and simply existent phenomena" (AC 66–67).

Finally, Troeltsch severely criticizes the teleological aspect of the concept of evolutionary development. In particular, he doubts the notion that the universal principle operative in history attains absolute self-realization at a specifiable point within history. On logical grounds alone, it is premature to speculate about the final or perfect culmination of world history in time, given our present intermediate location within the historical process. Borrowing Hegel's famous phrase from his *Grunlinien der Philosophie des Rechts*, he notes that despite occasionally urgent intimations of history's ending, the actual close of the historical process must precede any speculation regarding the meaning and significance of all that has transpired in history up until the present moment. For this reason, it is impossible to identify any religion as absolute while history is still in progress. "One senses that he is indeed oriented toward a goal, but he feels that until the end of history is reached, he ought not to speak of an absolute religion but should await it in close conjunction with the end of all history. There must be complete twilight before the owl of Minerva can begin its flight in the land of the realized absolute principle" (AC 69).[8]

In addition to arguing in principle against the notion of absolute realization, Troeltsch objects more concretely to identifying the absolute religion with any particular historical phenomenon. Troeltsch's appreciation of the individuality of all historical phenomena eliminates the possibility that any such entity could represent the perfect and complete manifestation of the universal principle supposedly underlying world history.[9] The modern understanding of history knows "no absolute realization of such a universal principle within the context of history where, as a matter of fact, only phenomena that are uniquely defined and limited and thus possess individual character are brought forth at any point" (AC 67).[10] From Troeltsch's historicist perspective, moreover, the interpretation of Christianity in particular as the absolute religion is especially erroneous. At precisely this point "the impossibility of uniting a theoretically conceived universal principle with a concrete, individual, historical configuration becomes directly discernible" (AC 70). Research into the origins and early history of primitive Christianity conducted by the *religionsgeschichtliche Schule* with which Troeltsch was indirectly associated disclosed the intimate involvement of the Christian religion with its immediate historical environment. This milieu included the thought-world of apocalyptic Judaism, the diverse philosophical and ethical systems of Greece and Rome, and the numerous cultic and mythological groupings of the ancient Near East. It was therefore apparent to Troeltsch that since its inception, Christianity must be regarded as a syncretistic product of quite specific historical factors and conditions, "bearing the stamp of a definite period of history" (AC 79). It is "evident that Christianity in every age, and particularly in its period of origin, is a genuinely historical phenomenon—new, by and large, in its consequences, but profoundly and radically conditioned by the historical situation and environment in which it found itself as well as by the relations it entered into in its further development" (AC 70).[11] Thus, without disparaging its historical significance or its status "under all circumstances [as] an eminent religious truth" (AC 70), Troeltsch insisted that the Christian religion must always be recognized as "a thoroughly concrete, limited, and conditioned movement" (AC 71). It emerged from, and developed within, a definite framework of cultural, social, and historical interrelationships. As Troeltsch concludes regarding the alleged uniqueness of the Christian religion from the perspective of the evolutionary apologetic, "nowhere is Christianity the absolute religion, an utterly unique species free of the historical conditions that comprise its environment at any given time. Nowhere is it the changeless, exhaustive, and unconditioned realization of that which is conceived as the universal principle of religion" (AC 71).

Troeltsch's Solution to the Problem of Absoluteness

Troeltsch's extensive critique of both the supernatural and the evolutionary theories of the absoluteness of Christianity led him to irrevocable negative assessments of these apologetic strategies. In his view, it is impossible to prove the absoluteness of Christianity either in opposition to historical thinking (as the former attempted to do) or, indeed, even in alliance with the modern idea of history (as the latter tried to accomplish). For Troeltsch, modern historical thought has demonstrated decisively that Christianity, like all other cultural and religious systems, is a thoroughgoing historical phenomenon. It is therefore a completely relative one.

> The Christian religion is in every moment of its history a purely historical phenomenon, subject to all the limitations to which any individual historical phenomenon is exposed, just like the other great religions. It is to be investigated, in every moment of its history, by the universal, verified methods of historical research. . . . If one should wish to say "Christianity is a relative phenomenon," there is no reason to object to this, for the historical and the relative are identical. Acknowledgement of this proposition can be evaded only by one who has deliberately or instinctively thrown up a bulwark to defend Christianity from the modern study of history. [AC 85]

For Troeltsch, however, recognizing the historically relative status of the Christian religion does not necessarily entail, as many dread, a state of normative chaos. In such a state the absence of any absolute value orientation undermines the establishment or affirmation of any ideals and standards by which to live amid the great abundance of such forms generated by history. On the contrary, according to Troeltsch, relativism necessitates not the disavowal of all values, but only an acknowledgment of their situational character.

> Relativity simply means that all historical phenomena are unique, individual configurations acted on by influences from a universal context that comes to bear on them in varying degrees of immediacy. . . . Relativity does not mean, however, the denial of the values that appear in these individual configurations, that are oriented in the same direction, that have the

power to encounter and influence one another, and that as a result of such interaction lead men to discern their inner truth and necessity and thus make a choice among them. [AC 89]

Stated in positive terms, what is demanded by relativism is conceptual clarification regarding the signification of the term relative and the precise relationship between historical relativism and the actual acquisition of "simple normative value" (AC 57) (if not absolute normative truth). "What everything really depends on is what the concept 'relative' means and how it relates to the problem of acquiring criteria of value. We have already given an exact definition of the concept of the absolute; we must now discuss the concept of historical relativity and its relationship to the attaining of norms" (AC 86). One may, in fact, achieve this, in Troeltsch's view, by formulating a theoretical program which steers a middle course between two extremes: the absolutist positions rejected in the name of real history, and an unlimited relativism in which unmitigated normative anarchy prevails. As Troeltsch insists, "the problem faced by the modern approach to history is not that of making an either/or choice between relativism and absolutism but that of how to combine the two" (AC 90).

In the remaining chapters of *Die Absolutheit des Christentums*, Troeltsch charts precisely such a course. He outlines a three-part program for dealing critically and responsibly with the problem of historical relativism, and offers considerable practical guidance regarding its actual implementation. In terms of the heuristic categories employed in chapter 3, this program includes the following major components: (1) a turn to history, which recognizes and celebrates the relativities found there as the point of departure for acquiring normative beliefs and values; (2) a subjective turn, in which the final choice among the diverse norms identified by the historian depends upon a decisive act of the individual subject; and (3) a metaphysical turn, which recognizes an absolute element in history as its final goal, so affirming a divine dimension to history in conjunction with the merely relative phenomena otherwise discerned there. An examination of Troeltsch's proposed solution to the crisis of historical relativism also illuminates his continued indebtedness to certain elements of the Hegelian paradigm. These elements are retained by Troeltsch even as he vigorously renounces the evolutionary apologetic model associated with Hegel.

The Turn to History

As the initial step in establishing viable norms by which to live, Troeltsch recommends a full immersion in, and affirmation of, the multiplicity of history. Instead of rejecting the body of non-Christian history, as did the proponents of the supernatural apologetic, the modern-day observer must embrace the entirety of history, in the fashion of the advocates of the evolutionary apologetic. The art of empathic understanding allows us to adopt the standpoint of alien cultural and religious systems. By this means, historians are urged to identify and delineate the diverse value orientations which have emerged in the course of history. With bias toward none, and sympathy to all, they must strive diligently to measure and compare, as objectively as possible, the different historical forms of the religious life. As a result of their labors, the entire range of the religious history of humanity and the outstanding features of each religious tradition will be available for all to peruse and contemplate. For, as Troeltsch emphasizes, "it is of the very essence of historical thinking to mark out clearly the great value orientations that have been achieved in the course of history and by which our existence is upheld, and to look into the depths of their interrelationship" (AC 97–98).

The task of historical description, however, is less intimidating that it first seems. In actual practice, historians may restrict themselves to a manageable number of the world religions. In this way they may impose at least a partial check on the seemingly unlimited relativism from the side of the historical object. "It would be highly fallacious to think of historical relativism as if it involved a limitless number of competing values. On the contrary, experience shows that such values are exceedingly few in number and that disclosures of really new goals for the human spirit are rare indeed. . . . In the history of religions in particular, we find ourselves confronted not by a profusion of powerful religious forces, among which we would never be able to choose, but only by a few great orientations" (AC 92). In particular, one must consider only the positive historical religions "of ethical and spiritual greatness" (AC 92). All so-called primitive religions, as well as all pseudo-religious rational and philosophical systems, may be excluded. The net result of this winnowing process is that one is left merely with the Judeo-Christian heritage of the West, on the one hand, and the religions of India (Hinduism and its primary derivative, Buddhism), on the other hand, "orientations that have their counterpart in, and give support to, entire spheres of culture" (AC 93). By applying critical skills of research and investigation to them, the historian renders clear and comprehensible the essential features of those religious systems which fall within the scope of the historical horizon as delimited above. Such is the contribution of the scientific study of history to the attainment of normative value.

The Turn to the Subject

Historical description, however, is only the preliminary phase of Troeltsch's prescription for a proper response to the problem of historical relativism. It is a necessary but insufficient condition for the possibility of its solution. "The study of history is not of itself the obtaining of such norms but the ground from which they arise. Historically delineated and actual norms are not necessarily norms we should acknowledge as valid for ourselves; they are disclosures of that principle from which we evolve valid norms" (AC 105). Unfortunately, the obvious benefits reaped by extensive historical knowledge about the world religious traditions may be accompanied by the risk of normative paralysis. A full-fledged absorption in history's multiplicity may incapacitate one from distinguishing among more or less adequate alternatives. Thus, drawing on the findings of descriptive history but moving decidedly beyond the stage of objective assessment, historically minded individuals must ultimately take a position with regard to the diverse value orientations of history. Following upon the comparative observations made possible by empirical research into the most prominent manifestations of spiritual life, they must choose the system of religious ideals and norms that is most intellectually acceptable and emotionally satisfying. By this means, they may break the impasse with which they are faced. More specifically, this is accomplished by ranking the different religions according to a specific criterion of value drawn from the most important features of various historical religions to which one has access. Such a standard is neither intuitively obvious nor randomly selected. It is a product of specific historical circumstances and so protrudes objectively from history.[12] Perhaps more important, it is the result of personal choice and decision and so is subjectively extracted from history.

Such a criterion is . . . a matter of personal conviction and is in the last analysis admittedly subjective. However, there is no other way to obtain a criterion that will enable us to choose among competing historical values. It is, in short, a personal, ethically oriented, religious conviction acquired by comparison and evaluation. . . . It has its objective basis in a scrupulous survey of the major religious orientations, in unprejudiced hypothetical empathy, and in conscientious evaluation, but its ultimate determination remains a matter of personal, subjective, inner conviction. [AC 96–97]

Thus, the turn to the historical which initiated this gambit must inevitably be followed by a complementary turn to the subject. The neutrality of historical inquiry eventually yields to the partiality that accompanies all acts of human decision, as the individual selects the religious value system of his or her preference and relegates all remaining religious traditions to a position of secondary importance.[13]

Troeltsch affirms the necessity of individual decision making at this juncture. However, he notes that this choice need not be made by everyone. Although many are called, few are chosen to perform this task. The chosen few are those individuals who possess the right admixture of historical learning and religious and ethical sensibility. "The inner truth and force of their solution will convince others" (AC 97).

Troeltsch unhesitatingly includes himself in this category of select individuals. He therefore offers specific advice concerning the choice of a criterion by which to rank and assess the world religions. For Troeltsch, the principle of personalism, as manifested primarily in the historical religion of Christianity, must be acknowledged as the highest religious standard which has emerged thus far in history. "Among the great religions Christianity is in actuality the strongest and most concentrated revelation of personalistic religious apprehension" (AC 111–12). This emphasis is prominent in both its idea of God and its vision of human selfhood. In comparison especially to the religions of India, Christian theism offers "the purest and most profound idea of God" (AC 103) as a spiritual or supernatural being—a notion of God, in a sense, as the ultimate person. The Hindu religious tradition construes divinity as "pure, highest being, or the supreme order of the world" (AC 110), as "an impersonal, eternally existing thing, as an ultimate abstraction from the given and actual" (AC 110–11). Buddhism conceives the ultimate principle as non-being or the eternal void. The Christian religion alone affirms "the person-like character of God" (AC 112). According to Troeltsch, "only Christianity has disclosed a living deity who is act and will in contrast to all that is merely existent" (AC 114).[14] Furthermore, the Christian emphasis on personalistic values is reflected in the differences between Christianity and other world religions regarding the correlative doctrines of self and human redemption. Despite the antithesis found in the Hindu religion between the inferior/natural and the superior/spiritual selves, both religious traditions of India ultimately devalue the human self by construing salvation in terms of the merger of God and the soul "into one, absolutely indistinguishable unity" (AC 111) (Hinduism) or the total annihilation of the self (Buddhism). In contrast, the Christian religion affirms the intrinsic value and integrity of personal life in the realm of human being. Christianity envisions redemption as the transformation of the human soul, and its elevation above and beyond a life bound by sensuous and natural conditions, to a higher (or divine) realm of transcendent value. This alone succeeds in preserving, rather than obliterating, the finite self, and so successfully raises individuals "into the sphere of personality" (AC 110).[15]

Thus, in *Die Absolutheit des Christentums*, Troeltsch both addresses and tries to resolve the problem of acquiring simple normative value. On the basis of his own theoretical program, Troeltsch provides a rational argument that affirms Christianity as the highest religious truth discernible in history from among its rivals and competitors in the sphere of the world religions. "The personalistic redemption-religion of Christianity is the highest and most significantly developed world of religious life that we know" (AC 117). Thus, Troeltsch substantially agrees with his theological predecessors regarding the supreme position of Christianity. However, the grounds for his own affirmation of Christianity's superiority have shifted dramatically from those of previous theological models. For Troeltsch, the assertion that Christianity is the highest religious truth known to humankind is no longer the by-product of the apologetic theories of earlier generations. These theories, as we have seen, attempted to validate Christianity based on ahistorical theoretical concepts or principles, such as miracles or metaphysically imbued notions of evolutionary development. Rather, within the schema outlined by Troeltsch, the normativeness of the Christian religion is derived directly from the history of religions itself. Within this history, Christianity (along with all other religious traditions) is inextricably located. By virtue of an immediate encounter with the relativities of history that is terminated only by a confessional act of the individual, one may affirm normative value within the limitations of historical relativism demanded by the modern world. This encounter points Troeltsch directly to a de facto recognition of the conditional absoluteness of Christianity.

> This is our situation, and only in this sense is it possible to affirm the "absoluteness of Christianity." This judgment issues from a joining together of absolute decision in the present with an interpretation of the developmental process that affirms historical relativity. It cannot emerge from repeated demonstrations of how Christianity, taken as an isolated object, produces an impression of absolute miracle, nor can it be deduced from the developmental process as a certain and verifiable law. . . . The "absoluteness" to which this inquiry has led us is simply the highest value discernible in history and the certainty of having found the way that leads to perfect truth. [AC 117–18]

Such a claim has obvious pragmatic benefits to the Christian faithful. It can never, however, have the unfailing certainty which previous apologetic strategies putatively possessed. First of all, in Troeltsch's view, the affirmation of the supreme validity of the Christian religion must always recognize that Christianity, in all circumstances, is never anything other than "a completely historical phenomenon" (AC 108). As Troeltsch never tires of repeating,

> By the same token it must not be forgotten that this revelation of the highest, purest, and most powerful religious life is a historical reality with all the individual and temporal limitations that apply to historical phenomena, and that it must retain these limitations no matter what form it takes on this earth. . . . Faith may regard Christianity . . . as a heightening of the religious standard in terms of which the inner life of man will continue to exist. But we cannot and must not regard it as an absolute, perfect, immutable truth. [AC 114–15]

Furthermore, this conclusion regarding the tentative nature of the truth of Christianity is ratified by the eschatological teachings of Christianity itself. These teachings affirm that the final manifestation of divine truth awaits the judgment that will take place at the close of human history. Such a doctrine asserts that "absolute truth belongs to the future and will appear in the judgment of God at the cessation of earthly history" (AC 115). "Thus," as Troeltsch continues, "even on its own premises, the absolute lies beyond history and is a truth that in many respects remains veiled" (AC 115). For the modern mind, Christianity is neither the perfect nor the final manifestation of religion in world history. Hence, while we may recognize with zeal its special status as the highest religious value for humanity, our acknowledgment of its absoluteness can never be more than a modest proposal.

The Metaphysical Turn

In the final analysis, Troeltsch denies in *Die Absolutheit des Christentums* that "absolute, unchanging value, conditioned by nothing temporal" (AC 90) may be discerned within history. However, he does not refute the reality of an absolute dimension to history. Indeed, as we have seen in chapter 3, Troeltsch adopted in his earlier writings a fundamentally metaphysical interpretation of the historical process. This reading of history posited the divine Reason as operative during its course as the ultimate guarantor of the temporal values found there. So, too, in *Die Absolutheit,* Troeltsch's theoretical program to resolve the problem of historical relativism includes a comparable turn to the metaphysical. Such a turn entails a shift in his mode of argument from mere historical description to explicitly philosophical speculation concerning the ultimate pattern and meaning of history. Borrowing once again from the Hegelian paradigm, Troeltsch suggests that the realm of history includes, in addition to the various temporally conditioned value formations which are found there, the presence and reality of an absolute factor.

What, more precisely, is the relationship between this absolute core of history and the historical process itself? In direct contrast to Hegel's philosophy of history, which posited the full realization of this Absolute within history, Troeltsch insists that the Absolute exists in some fundamental way beyond or outside history as its common goal or final telos. Troeltsch's argument in *Die Absolutheit* suggests that the claim that we may find the Absolute in its full and pristine form in the course of history is delusory. Nevertheless, Troeltsch is convinced that there indeed exists a transcendent dimension to history, beyond that which is empirically accessible. Such a conviction is better expressed in temporal rather than spatial terms. It takes the form of the belief that the Absolute is discernible at the end of earthly history, rather than within the historical process. By re-locating the Absolute to the indefinite future, Troeltsch readily admits that its existence cannot be a matter of scientific demonstration. It can be apprehended indirectly "only by presentiment and faith" (AC 90). Regardless of the mode by which it is accessible, however, Troeltsch in *Die Absolutheit des Christentums* retains the metaphysical assumptions regarding history introduced in his earlier essays considered in chapter 3.

But despite its fundamental relationship of transcendence to world history, the Absolute, according to Troeltsch, is in some sense immanent to history as well. "Though transcending history in its changeless perfection, this goal can be manifested within history at different points along the ascent toward the higher orientations of life in ways adapted to each historical situation and its presuppositions" (AC 95). While never realizing itself "as far as the sum total of its content is concerned" (AC 100), the Absolute indeed from time to time discloses itself, however partially and conditionally, amid the diversity and multiplicity of history. Under all circumstances, of course, these historical formations "remain individual and temporally conditioned entities throughout every moment of their existence" (AC 90). Thus they may never be seen as anything other than approximations of absolute value. Yet, as partial or temporary revelations of that which is, by definition, itself "the principle of normativeness and universal validity" (AC 99), these values partake of the ontological reality manifested within them. They thereby may be regarded as something more than merely relative values.

> History is a unique sphere of knowledge because it is the sphere of the individual and nonrecurrent. But within the individual and nonrecurrent, there is something universally valid . . . which makes itself known at the same time. The problem is to hold these two elements together in the right relation. [AC 106]

The problem is to define the scope of the relative and individual with ever increasing exactness and to understand with ever increasing comprehensiveness the universally valid that works teleologically within history. Then we will see that the relative contains an indication of the unconditional. In the relative we will find a token of the absolute that transcends history. [AC 106]

Additionally, Troeltsch's view that the divine is located in some sense out in front of history allows us to conceptualize the dynamic interrelationships to be found among the value configurations within history. As the transcendent goal of history, the Absolute exerts a teleological pull on the historical process. As a result, the movement of history gradually approaches, or converges upon, its final goal, if only asymptotically. In this light, one may discern, amid the flux of history, a pattern of movement, whereby its "individual preparatory forms" (AC 98) may be arranged according to the approximate degree to which they approach this final telos. In so claiming, Troeltsch reaffirms the notion that every moment in the historical process is of intrinsic value. In and of itself it is a manifestation of the Absolute. "Of course every new stage in the revelatory process must for its part stand as a historically constituted realization and precursor of the ultimate goal of man, and to that extent it is, as Ranke was fond of saying, 'directly related to God'" (AC 99). Nonetheless, the notion that history in some way compulsively moves forward toward an ultimate goal, even as that goal stands inescapably beyond the historical process, allows for the legitimate retrieval, in Troeltsch's philosophical interpretation of history, of the notion of evolutionary development associated with Hegel. This notion serves as an appropriate category by which to comprehend this forward movement of history. "At the same time, however, each stage [of history] also affords a foundation essential to all further development. The point is to work out on this basis increasingly extensive and penetrating—even if always individual and temporally conditioned—explications of the goal toward which mankind is directed" (AC 99).

Troeltsch emphatically notes that such a retrieval is not to be confused with the unqualified reappropriation of theories of development previously rejected by Troeltsch—for sound historical reasons—in his critique of the evolutionary apologetic discussed above.

> To be sure, the attempt to identify this concept of a goal with a generative, causal law has to be abandoned; so too with the attempt to compute absolute realization from an empirical series of qualitative gradations and from what is alleged to be a historically demonstrable exhausting of its inner principle. The doctrine that stages of development can be calculated according to a strict law—the Hegelian dialectic—has to be given up. . . . It must not be maintained that reality is panlogistic and monistic in character. Just as what is universally valid is not a law that calls the whole of reality into being, so evolutionary development is not mere successive realization of an idea. Evolutionary development means, rather, the eruption—at coexisting but discrete points—of dynamic orientations directed toward the absolute goal of the human spirit. [AC 100–101]

But even in the face of his decisive rejection of the "speculative concept of evolution" (AC 102), it is still possible, in light of his operative philosophical presuppositions, to speak of "the upward course of history" (AC 103) or of its various "higher and lower stages" (AC 113). As a result, Troeltsch preserves at least a quasi-developmental view of the historical process, reminiscent of Hegel's schema of the evolutionary movement of history. This suggests a second element of congruence between Troeltsch and the Hegelian paradigm.

Finally, Troeltsch's ability and willingness to perceive history in terms of a "natural gradation" (AC 98) once again introduces the theoretical issue of whether, and to what extent, any individual historical phenomenon may occupy a privileged position within this developmental framework. Troeltsch unequivocally answers that the Christian religion is precisely such a phenomenon. For him, its affirmation of personalistic religious values, as we have seen, qualifies it as the most adequate expression of religious values in history. It also qualifies as both the "culmination point" and "the convergence point of all the developmental tendencies that can be discerned in religion. It may therefore be designated, in contrast to other religions, as the focal synthesis of all religious tendencies and the disclosure of what is in principle a new way of life" (AC 114).

In keeping with conclusions stated in his earlier writings, Troeltsch did not intend such an affirmation as a reversion to previous claims of the Hegelian paradigm that Christianity is in some way an absolute phenomenon. Christianity is never liberated from its historical limitations by virtue of its special place in the progressive movement of history. "That this new life [disclosed by Christianity] is not synonymous with the realization of a universal principle of religion established by abstraction need not be repeated. Christianity is the culmination point not despite but in terms of its particularity and distinctive features, and on this basis the goal of religion undergoes decisively new determinations" (AC 114). Nevertheless, despite its thoroughly historical character, Troeltsch's conviction was that the Christian religion somehow stands apart from the remainder of history. It does so, moreover, in a way which partially resembles its special status within Hegel's evolutionary apologetic for the absoluteness of Christianity.

Given Troeltsch's affirmation of the open-ended quality of the historical process, is Christianity a religion that will remain normative for the indefinite future? According to Troeltsch, the Christian religion is, at least in principle, capable of being eclipsed. Because of its constitutively historical makeup, one cannot claim with any great assurance that it will continue as the zenith of religious development until such time as the historical process finally meets its transcendent goal. "It cannot be proved with absolute certainty that Christianity will always remain the final culmination point, that it will never be surpassed" (AC 114–15). Nevertheless, in practice, one may assert that its longevity and the inherent strength of its inner qualities, in all probability, guarantee with reasonable certitude that Christianity will persist indefinitely as the culminating point of the religious history of humankind that is known to us. This guarantee holds even if it is impossible to rule out the abstract possibility of further revelations.

> Christianity is the pinnacle of religious development thus far and the basis and presupposition for every distinct and meaningful development in man's religious life in the future. There is no probability that it will ever be surpassed or cut off from its historical foundations as far as our historical vision can reach. That is the result we have arrived at so far in this approach which has taken historical relativity into account and has also been shown to satisfy the religious need for certainty of communion with God and for assurance of salvation. [AC 131]

Troeltsch's Relation to Hegel in *Die Absolutheit des Christentums*

The foregoing analysis demonstrates that Troeltsch's relationship to the thought of Hegel in *Die Absolutheit des Christentums* is crucial to his attempt to certify the viability of religious norms in light of modern historical thinking. On the one hand, Troeltsch is sceptical of the usefulness of the evolutionary theory for the absoluteness of the Christian religion associated with Hegel for resolving the problem of historical relativism. In the name of real history, he dissects and examines critically the main components of this theory. In each case Troeltsch shows its fundamental incompatibility with what, at least in his mind, is a more adequate understanding of the real nature of historical life. The essential features of this critique require no repeating here. It is sufficient to state that in spite of its relative adequacy in comparison to its supernatural counterpart, Troeltsch unequivocally rejects the Hegelian paradigm as a responsible solution to the central problematic with which Troeltsch himself was so passionately concerned in this text.

Nonetheless, Troeltsch's scepticism regarding the Hegelian paradigm is belied, at least in part, by the nature and degree to which certain features of this paradigm persist, albeit in modified form, within his own efforts to address historicism and its impact on religious values. Despite his self-conscious attempt to distance himself from the apologetic theory of his predecessor, Troeltsch incorporates several features of the paradigm within his own theoretical program—often in a less-than-subtle manner. Despite his own call for the full-bodied immersion in, and affirmation of, the relativities of history, Troeltsch appeals to a metaphysics of history, so intimately linked with Hegel, as an integral part of his efforts to confront the problem of historical relativism. For Troeltsch, as for Hegel, it is not enough soley to rely on the historical per se. Rather, both share the fundamental conviction that history contains a transhistorical dimension. This conviction provides the anchor to their respective efforts adequately to respond to this problem. We have also seen that Troeltsch rejects the concept of evolutionary development in the rigid form which it takes in the Hegelian dialectic of history and denies Hegel's claim for Christianity's absoluteness as the logical conclusion of the latter's philosophy of the history of religion. This does not prevent him, however, from appropriating these features of Hegel's thought, in a manner in keeping with his more historicist standpoint. To be sure, Troeltsch's claim to see in history the semblance of a developmental process, and his contention that Christianity represents the culmination of this pattern of historical movement, represent only formal equivalents of their counterparts within Hegel's vision of history. But these traces of the Hegelian paradigm within Troeltsch's theoretical framework are persuasive evidence of the survival of the paradigm, even in the midst of a theory ostensibly hostile to its claims and presuppositions.

In conclusion, then, Troeltsch's critical response to Hegel in *Die Absolutheit des Christentums* bears witness to the central thesis of this study as a whole: namely, that a relationship of complementarity exists between Troeltsch and one of his most important intellectual forerunners. Troeltsch's motives and reasons for rejecting the Hegelian paradigm are clearly stated in the course of *Die Absolutheit*, and so the moment of departure from Hegel is obvious. Yet the moment of retrieval is present as well, testifying to the irrepressibility of the paradigm within Troeltsch's thought. The degree to which Troeltsch's attempt to make sense of historical life continues to vary even more dramatically from Hegel's model of history, without forsaking it entirely, is the subject of chapter 5. In this chapter, Troeltsch's relation to Hegel during the last stages of his career will be investigated.

Historical Relativism and the Crisis of Cultural Values: Troeltsch's Critique of Hegel in *Der Historismus und seine Probleme*

This chapter inspects Troeltsch's critical investigation of Hegel's philosophy of history, as he conducts this examination in *Der Historismus und seine Probleme.* In this text, Troeltsch again addresses the crisis of historical relativism, although he has widened the range of his inquiry to include cultural values as a whole.[1] His response to the problem of historicism is initially couched in terms of a systematic philosophical treatment of the nature of history. This treatment is intended to disengage historical thinking from the throes of its main nemesis: naturalism. In the course of this enterprise, Troeltsch pursued a running debate with many of "the great representative authorities" (GS 3:viii) in the Western philosophical tradition in order to clarify his own position on the matters taken up therein.[2] Much of *Der Historismus* is therefore an extended commentary upon the views concerning certain pivotal issues in the philosophy of history that are held by a wide range of thinkers. This spectrum figuratively extends "from Voltaire and Herder to Comte and Hegel" (GS 3:vii) but also includes others of varying intellectual stature. In addition, Troeltsch's theoretical reflection on historicism hints of a pragmatic solution to the problem of relativism in the form of a synthesis of cultural values, grounded on the formal logic of history, which he elucidates at great length in this massive volume. In the context of these ruminations on the crisis of historical thought and values, written and compiled late in his academic career, Troeltsch offers his final critique of the central elements of the Hegelian paradigm of history.[3]

The Present-Day Crisis of History

In the years immediately following the first World War, Troeltsch perceived that Western culture was poised at the brink of a significant transition insofar as historical thinking was concerned. In his view, however, this crisis had to do "less with the historical investigation of scholars and specialists than with the historical thought of mankind in general" (GS 3:1). Technical historical research—characterized by the critical examination and interpretation of historical sources and the cautious reconstruction of past events—was in his day in a state of relatively good health. Despite the existence of certain problems endemic to any science approaching its maturity, Troeltsch notes that, since the early nineteenth century, "its achievements have grown to an admirable breadth, fullness, and keenness" (GS 3:2), and the skillful and impartial application of its basic methods and techniques has made of historical study "an approximately exact science" (GS 3:1).[4]

But, according to Troeltsch, if the true locus of this metamorphosis is not the sphere of the empirical science of history, "the crisis is therefore all the more severe in *the general philosophical foundations and elements of historical thinking*" (GS 3:4). Stated more simply, it is "the problem of the *meaning and essence of historicism generally*" (GS 3:102). In particular, Troeltsch felt that the reorientation of historical thought then underway was best understood as the transition from a view of history captive to a naturalistic conception of the world and its philosophical presuppositions toward an understanding of history liberated from these fetters. Since its inception in the eighteenth century, the philosophy of history had shared center stage with the natural sciences and mathematics and their philosophical treatment. Often adversaries in the Western tradition, rarely allies, naturalism and historicism and their internecine debate in many ways set the parameters within which the understanding of self and world in recent centuries has been shaped. Indeed, "the struggle between philosophy of nature and philosophy of history has been one of the great themes of the modern spirit, one that has been, and is even today, elaborated with continually changing points of emphasis" (GS 3:11).[5] That this debate in his own day appeared to have reached a decisive turning point, however, impelled Troeltsch himself to address this crisis in *Der Historismus und seine Probleme*. There he joined forces with those philosophically kindred spirits in their emancipation of historical thought from the derogatory associations of a bad historicism founded on a naturalistic understanding of history.

By way of definition, Troeltsch states that naturalism must be understood "as the connection, embracing all of reality, that seeks to formulate laws disregarding everything qualitative and all immediate experience. It is the foundation of a system of quantitative laws of relation, as much as possible mathematically expressible, beneath the everyday experience of ordinary consciousness. It is the representation of the material images of experience and their interrelation by means of mathematical formulae that proceed from the essence of pure space" (GS 3:103). In and of itself, naturalism is not a maleficent force in the history of ideas. Indeed, the success of the various natural sciences and their methods and interpretive principles has been nothing less than spectacular and deserves our praise and admiration. Nevertheless, despite the momentous achievements of the natural sciences, Troeltsch observes that since the rise of modern historical thinking, the attempt to understand history in philosophical terms requires that we recognize, establish, and rescue the autonomy of the historical realm in relation to the world of nature. From time to time this effort has taken precise philosophical shape in response to the incursion of the naturalistic worldview into the historical sphere. In terms of methodology, this encroachment has manifested itself as the inappropriate utilization of the procedures and governing assumptions of the natural sciences as the proper means to understand the world of history. All philosophical reflection upon history thereby becomes subordinate to natural scientific modes of inquiry. These include, especially, the assumption that the world of nature is a closed system of interrelationships, a mechanistic view of biological evolution, and the application of the principle of a universally valid natural causality as the fundamental explanatory principle operative in the physical world. Expressed in ontological terms, the most threatening implication of the naturalistic worldview has been the periodic emergence of a materialistic metaphysic. This metaphysic has the propensity to confuse the realms of history and nature and to reduce all historical life to the status of "a curious, isolated epiphenomenon of the natural processes that alone bring to pass reality strictly speaking" (GS 3:88).

In his own era, however, Troeltsch detected intimations of a reorientation of the philosophical treatment of history away from the biases of naturalism. This revival took the form of the vigorous reawakening of the philosophy of history then underway. It was primarily inaugurated, if not completely brought to fruition, by the philosophical labor of neo-Kantianism and its strident reaction against the "methodological monism" (GS 3:24) promulgated by naturalism. In the eyes of its most representative figures (notably, Wilhelm Dilthey and Heinrich Rickert), it was necessary to affirm the logical independence and uniqueness of the social and cultural sciences versus the natural sciences, without disparaging the latter's achievements.[6] In so doing, moreover, it became possible to affirm the uniqueness of historical reality as a self-determining sphere of life in contrast to natural reality. Indeed, it became possible to assert the complete disparity between history and nature.[7] Only in this way, in their view, could history be protected from the deadly naturalization of thought and allowance made for a philosophical analysis of the historical world which would do it justice.

Such, in brief, were the philosophical contributions of Troeltsch's neo-Kantian contemporaries to the ongoing combat between the philosophy of history and its great antagonist. In the wake of their vigorous opposition to the omnicompetence of the natural-scientific method, Troeltsch stepped through the door opened by neo-Kantian theory and engaged in a sprawling philosophical investigation into the nature of history, based on mutually shared assumptions regarding its autonomous methodology and logic. Troeltsch initiated and implemented this task intermittently throughout *Der Historismus und seine Probleme*. In this text he attempted to define the contours of the historical world, and, in particular, the characteristic features of history which distinguished it from nature. This endeavor took concrete form in Troeltsch's efforts to identify and clarify the two fundamental categories of history, located respectively on its synchronic and diachronic axes: the historical object and historical becoming. Accordingly, I next discuss Troeltsch's conceptualization of the underlying rationality of history. In so doing, I devote special attention to how Troeltsch's articulation of the formal logic of history frames his critical response to the way these categories are envisioned within the Hegelian paradigm discussed and analyzed in chapter 2 above.

The Formal Logic of History
The Category of Individual Totality

As Troeltsch indicates in chapter 1 of *Der Historismus*, the attempt to formulate a philosophical model of the structure of historical life is not begun in a vacuum. Rather, the foundational concepts employed in any theoretical account of history must be derived from "the actual procedure of historians describing concrete history" (GS 3:30). Thus we are directed to the concept of individuality, or more precisely, that of individual totality, as the most fundamental category of historical study. This concept, therefore, is the most appropriate point of departure for a formal analysis of its underlying logic.

> Here one must emphasize fundamentally that real history is, according to general practice, the concrete, vivid description of the always-individual formations of history and that no practitioner [of history] has ever been able completely to avoid this. What importance those generalizing disciplines, especially sociology, ethology, and typology, may always have for the study of history, they have, up to now, never been able to dislodge and replace description. This is quite natural, since what is really interesting and belongs to reality proper, lies in the vivid, infinitely diverse happening. [GS 3:30]

Troeltsch deliberately used the term *totality* to designate the objective entities found in the sphere of history in order to distinguish his own view of historical reality from that of the natural sciences. According to the naturalistic perspective, the universe is composed of essentially homogeneous constituent particles. These may be either units of matter (atoms or chemical elements) or of energy. In contrast, the concept of a totality suggests an aggregate structure, consisting of a "life-unity" (GS 3:33) of assorted or heterogeneous parts. These parts are drawn in variable measure from both the "spiritual" or "psychical" realm and "pure natural substrata" (GS 3:33), and are associated, or coinhere, with one another in a somewhat loose and ever-shifting manner. Conceived in this way, the basic object of history is never less than a complex or composite entity. It is not dissoluble in any way to material of a more primordial nature.

Troeltsch's view of the historical object benefits an understanding of history that respects its uniqueness and autonomy relative to nature. Conceiving the primary phenomena of history as composite *Gestalten* fosters and protects the individual character of all historical entities. Calling attention to their internal distinctions ensures that historical forms may not be reduced to elements of identical substance or essence, as are found in nature. Troeltsch's vision of the objects of history as amalgamations or constellations of many distinct parts guarantees the idiosyncratic character of any single object, by which it distinguishes and separates itself from other equally individual formations.

By construing this object as a complex manifold of diverse elements, furthermore, Troeltsch regards historical individuals as collectivities or groups, rather than as particular human beings. Although ordinary usage of the term suggests otherwise, Troeltsch argues, as did Hegel before him, that the true individuals of history are those entities whose internal breadth and depth, to varying degrees, transcend and encapsulate singular persons. In a further echo of Hegel, Troeltsch proposes that the individual collectivities most central to historical study are the various nations and states of history. Empirical historical investigation is not restricted to these suprapersonal entities. It may be directed to "totalities arranged below, above, or beside" (GS 3:35) them—aggregates organized according to economic, sociological, cultural, ideational, and geographic, as well as political, variables. In any event, however, the historical observer can recognize the general principle of unity of any such totality by the inner structure and content of meaning and value, immanent to a specific individual whole, which resides there. Historical things are, first and foremost, cohesive totalities of signification. On the basis of the system of unified meanings which they include, incorporate, or embody, they may be identified and set apart from each other.

In the opening chapter of *Der Historismus*, Troeltsch elaborates upon the nature of the individual totality in terms of a wide range of auxiliary categories intended to clarify and expand upon its central import and significance. The most important of these categories is what Troeltsch refers to as the originality of the historical object. "In this concept of the individual totality, which does not at all refer primarily to biography and the single person . . . the concept of *originality and uniqueness* is . . . included. This particular principle exists in something that can not be derived and explained any further, that one can understand sympathetically but cannot deduce" (GS 3:38).

As we have seen in the preceding chapter, the concept of originality is especially crucial for an adequate philosophical account of history, because it illumines an additional way in which the object of historical life may be decisively distinguished from its counterpart in the natural realm. If the individual totalities of history are not reducible to simpler, naturalistic elements, neither are they deducible from any one (or several) antecedent factors or conditions. In the physical world, a doctrine of strict causal equivalence is everywhere operative. What appears in nature is qualitatively similar to its prior cause. In contrast, no such universal law of monistic causality applies in history, where cause and effect are always incommensurable. What emerges in the historical sphere is indubitably shaped and influenced by the nexus of factors and conditions (both natural and historical) from which it arises. It does so, however, spontaneously—mysteriously, if not miraculously. It is in no way explainable or derivable, in a manner of one-to-one correspondence, by means of a set of environmental or situational variables. Summarizing the notion of causality of a sort that is most relevant to historical explanation, Troeltsch states that historical understanding entails

> no abrogation whatever of the concept of causality. Everything indeed comes to pass by the impetus and combination of all kinds of conditions and causes, and the sympathetic investigator can even re-experience the entire causal process in himself. But this is a fundamental distinction over against the natural scientific concept of causality, which is based on the equivalence of cause and effect, on quantitative similarity. Historical causality is oriented to dissimilarity, to an understanding of the occurrence of the new and the augmentation of reality. The rationalism of the natural sciences proceeds to the greatest possible identity, the understanding of history to this incalculable newness and the reality of that which is produced. [GS 3:48–49]

For Troeltsch, then, history with its revised conception of the causal relationship between or among objects is unequivocally the realm of the qualitatively new, the constantly surprising, and the substantively unique. History is not without its interconnections and its regularities. What erupts there, however, always entails an enlargement of reality. It is never a mere reshaping or restructuring of preexistent elements according to immutable laws of nature. "On this originality . . . rests the real charm and content of historical life, the inner freedom and independence from mere conditions and surroundings, antecedents and influences. So far as these also are always of importance and have an effect, they never exhaust what takes shape out of and in them" (GS 3:39).

The liberation of the historical object from laws of strict causal connection highlights, in turn, its final distinguishing mark—the radical contingency of the individual totalities of history. If that which is bodied forth in history cannot be explained deductively by the law of cause and effect, then what emerges there may never be construed as logically necessary. It is instead always and inexplicably the product of chance. According to Troeltsch, all historical objects are essentially coincidences—the issue of "the cross-fertilization of diverse, heterogeneous systems of law lacking a common root" (GS 3:51). The latter intersect or intermesh at a particular moment in time, for no foreseeable reason, then diverge again in an equally unpredictable manner. As a means to attain some cognitive control over the role of chance in human experience, the apparent arbitrariness of history has, at times, been translated into various theological notions, for example, doctrines of providence or predestination. Indeed, Troeltsch asserts metaphorically that "grace and election are the secret and essence of history" (GS 3:101). The use of such language tends to go beyond "the boundary of pure history" (GS 3:53). Nevertheless, it points to an urgent need on the part of the human victims or beneficiaries of the contingencies of life to affirm some degree of logical understanding, if not mastery, of this unyielding feature of historical existence.

TROELTSCH'S CRITIQUE OF HEGEL'S CONCEPT OF INDIVIDUALITY

Troeltsch's theoretical analysis in *Der Historismus* of the individual totalities of history is principally set forth in counterpoise to an understanding of the historical object espoused by the natural sciences. However, it also sets the stage for his critique of the concept of individuality found in the Hegelian paradigm, the alternative philosophical solution to "the problem of the individual" (GS 3:132) of most relevance to the goals of this chapter.

In chapter 2 I discussed in detail the notion that what is historically unique occupies a central place within Hegel's philosophy of history. It is a cardinal tenet of Hegel's vision of history that an intimate association exists between concrete history and the divine Idea indwelling in the historical process. On the basis of the fundamental metaphysical presuppositions which pervade his philosophy of history, of course, Hegel regards the fullness of history in its entirety as a product of the self-unfolding power of the divine. More specifically, Hegel construes the various individuals of history—especially its great collective wholes—as nothing less than discrete ontological manifestations of the divine Reason. They are the explicit historical material employed from time to time by the World Spirit in its efforts to arrive at its final desideratum: self-knowledge. As a result, Hegel's vision of world history comprehends the relationship between the individuals of history and the divine Idea as a thoroughly symbiotic one. On the one hand, the individual totalities of history are imbued with a special ontological significance in their capacity as embodiments of the Absolute. By virtue of their unique participation in the life of the divine Reason, as its manifestations, the finite individuals of history attain a status which transcends that of mere historical entities. They become transfigured for the world-historical philosopher who has eyes to see. Yet, on the other hand, this relationship is equally beneficial to the divine Spirit. In the framework of the Hegelian paradigm, the Absolute becomes incarnate in history by actualizing itself through the medium of history's collectivities. It is only by so doing that the process of self-manifestation in history is effected by the World Spirit, the process which ultimately culminates in Spirit's achievement of its final goal of self-consciousness. Thus, Hegel's treatment of the category of individuality ostensibly represents a disclosure of the powerful significance of real historical objects. By positing a close interrelationship between ordinary history and its metaphysical dimension, the Hegelian paradigm, among all interpretations of historical individuality, appears to be the apogee of an appreciation for the contingent and the unique.

Nevertheless, despite Hegel's efforts to unite and hold together that which is historically individual and the suprahistorical Absolute, Troeltsch contends that Hegel fails to do so in a way that respects simultaneously both dimensions of reality.[8] Where Hegel postulates a facile relationship between the Infinite and the finite, both endorsing the supremacy of the transhistorical realm and affirming the value of what resides in the realm of history itself, Troeltsch discerns only tension and contradiction. Where Hegel sees the ultimate convergence of these two concepts, Troeltsch sees in Hegel's thought only their inevitable divergence from each other.

At the outset of his critique of the Hegelian paradigm in chapter 2 of *Der Historismus*, Troeltsch suggests that, at least in theory, linking the concept of individuality with the notion of the divine Reason is detrimental to both parties to this relationship. Troeltsch applauds Hegel's frequently incisive and penetrating interpretations of concrete history—its nation-states, philosophical systems, religious traditions, etc.—as they are set forth in various places within the Hegelian corpus.[9] Troeltsch notes, however, that insofar as history is construed primarily as the self-unfolding or self-explication of the eternal Reason, undue emphasis is placed on the divine or rational element in world history. This risks reducing or minimizing the importance of the concrete or individual element that constitutes history as it really is. "If what is rational and conceptual is taken strictly in its abstract sense and its only logically-stipulated explication, then a monstrous assault on real history results, in spite of Hegel's profound glimpse into the essence of concrete-individual historical structures" (GS 3:130). Conversely, according to Troeltsch, the relationship between the finite and the Infinite is equally severable, if primary stress is placed on the side of concrete history. The ontological connection between the collectivities of history and the divine Idea which permeates them is what joins these historical formations together in a singular process. Apart from this joinder, the individual totalities of history are vulnerable to hypostatization in a thoroughly nominalistic fashion, such that all linkage with the transhistorical realm is torn asunder. "But if one takes away only the method of extracting from isolated historical structures their occasionally uniform conceptual sense and in such a way—to use Hegel's words—determine the 'principle' of Hellenism, of Roman law, of Catholicism, of Germanic life, etc., then these concepts at once become individual concepts and destroy every connection with an a priori construable, uniform, normal idea of historical values" (GS 3:130–31). It is Troeltsch's view, therefore, that despite Hegel's good intentions, he could not consistently join together the realms of the universal divine Idea and the historically particular. The bond which ostensibly links these two elements is, indeed, a double bind, in which their union is both espoused and undermined at one and the same time. "The contradiction between the rational Idea and individual-concrete history persists therefore even in Hegel, despite the conceivably most intimate association of the two. If one devotes himself to real history, the Idea disappears; if one constructs history from the Idea, real history disappears" (GS 3:131).

Nonetheless, despite these theoretical failings of the Hegelian paradigm, in practice its inadequacies belong exclusively on the side of Hegel's inability to affirm the ultimate value and significance of real, concrete history. For Troeltsch, Hegel's apparent effort to glorify and exalt the individuals of history as particular manifestations of the Absolute in service of a higher cause disappoints. Troeltsch concludes that Hegel does not make what is individual as such the object of his thinking, and so fails to value concrete history unequivocally in its own right. Paradoxically, by virtue of their linkage with the transhistorical Idea, the individual totalities of history are, in Troeltsch's view, ultimately deprived of any intrinsic worth. As a result, Hegel's underlying attitude of indifference toward the contingencies of history is revealed. In the final analysis, the relationship within the framework of the Hegelian paradigm between the World Spirit and historical individuals becomes less one of symbiosis and more an uneasy partnership between nonequals. For Hegel, the true import of the individuals of history is ultimately vitiated. Their functional value in the service of the divine renders them mere implements of the aims of Reason. They possess only passing (and not enduring) significance as humble points through which the divine life process moves.

> However high-mindedly and plastically [Hegel] was able to see and emphasize what is individual, it has for him a double meaning, exactly like his entire construction of the process. It appears sometimes as an inherently valuable, genuine concretion of the Absolute, with its own meaning and significance, and sometimes as a mere point of passage and support of the logical identity that moves through everything that is individual. It becomes the marionette and the material of the "cunning of Reason," which makes the great

passions, occupied apparently only with themselves, its means, known only to itself. Then, however, the individual, which at first seemed so powerfully and decisively as a concretion, evaporates and becomes an abstract isolation of a point of a process, a simple subjectivity. [GS 3:132]

In sum, then, Troeltsch believed that the characteristic individuality of the historical object, which he persistently labored in *Der Historismus* to affirm, was irrevocably sacrificed by Hegel, just as it was forsaken in the naturalistic understanding of history. According to Troeltsch, Hegel's seeming willingness to celebrate the significance of that which is historically individual is finally overridden by the emphasis which the Hegelian paradigm places on premises external to history. Hegel ascribes meaning to that which is individual in history only insofar as it mirrors suprahuman or transhistorical reality. He thus ultimately succeeds only in deriving the meaning of the world of contingency completely in terms of the divine ground of history. He thereby disparages the individual totalities of history, rather than recognizing their worth. Whatever his claims to the contrary, Hegel's philosophy of history, in Troeltsch's view, fails to bring history's concrete richness and diversity to bear on the divine life. The substantive value and content of history is finally dissolved in the Absolute, just as the proponents of naturalism would have the concrete individuality of history vanish into nature. Troeltsch himself was never willing totally to detach the realm of ordinary history from its metaphysical ingredients. However, he vigorously denied the rigid identification of the historically individual with any substance of another order which somehow stands behind it, whether it be the divine Reason or the realm of nature. He instead affirmed without qualification the historical object in all of its genuine originality, brute particularity, and stubborn uniqueness—traits which his formal analysis of the nature of historicism illuminates. While the objects of history may never be anything less than concrete individuals (as Troeltsch energetically asserts against naturalism), it is equally disastrous to claim, as did Hegel, that they are something more, whose latent significance goes beyond the merely historical.

The Concept of Historical Development

Troeltsch's theoretical analysis of history concerns itself, in the first instance, with explicating the fundamental objects of history. It is hardly limited, however, to an understanding of history merely in terms of the events or constellations of meaning that form its subject matter. On the contrary, Troeltsch's nuanced consideration of the individual totalities of history segues in *Der Historismus und seine Probleme* into an analysis of history as a temporal process. It is this dimension of history to which more than half of this volume is devoted. The transition from an examination of the historical object to an inquiry into the nature of historical becoming is easily made when one acknowledges that the various individual totalities of history are not frozen in time, as one might infer from the process of abstraction by which they are identified by the historian. They possess instead an inner dynamism or vitality which thrusts or impels them through time. The fundamental object of history "is constantly in motion, internally and in relation to other objects. It belongs to a continuous flow of becoming and must be so placed" (GS 3: 54).[10] In light, then, of the essentially dynamic nature of historical entities, any delineation of the structure of historical life must recognize the pattern of change or temporal movement endemic to history. Troeltsch characterizes this pattern as development, a category which he situates at the "center of the entire modern historicism" (GS 3:227).

In order to do justice to the notion of becoming as it is actually found in history, Troeltsch locates the concept of development between two main poles. On the one hand, he distinguishes historical development from the kind of change appropriate to nature. Historical development must possess a sufficient degree of fluidity, in contrast to the rigid chronological sequence which characterizes a naturalistic understanding of change. On the other hand, the process of historical becoming must also be differentiated from thoroughly random temporal movement, or pure flux. Historical development must hence possess a degree of continuity and never lapse into aimless motion.

As we have seen, Troeltsch's vision of historical reality explicitly rejects the principle of universal causality in order to affirm the uniqueness or originality of the historical object. Translated into terms of temporal process, the causal connection between phenomena may be expressed as a highly spatialized view of becoming. Troeltsch dismisses this concept of time with equal force. In his view, the application of strictly causal categories to an understanding of change inevitably but incorrectly subsumes temporality under categories of space. By envisioning the world as a nexus of events governed by the law of causality, as does the naturalistic perspective, one may analyze experience in terms of clear-cut, particular occurrences which correspond to the generic notions of cause and effect. Succession then becomes nothing more than the alignment or serial arrangement of these moments along a continuum. Temporally contiguous causes and effects are located in the appropriate chronological sequence, in order to illumine their positions relative to each other on the causal chain. As a result, however, development becomes nothing more than the imposition of the topography of cause and effect onto time, as the structural relationships governed by causality are mapped or plotted in a rigid, sequential order. In Troeltsch's view, however, this spatialized understanding of time does violence to historical time as it really is. Real history cannot be reduced to strictly demarcated, isolable moments that may be correlated to causal categories. Rather, it is more adequately construed as a highly fluid medium in which past, present, and future intersect or interpenetrate each other. In a view of temporality that has its roots in the Western tradition as far back as Book Eleven of Augustine's *Confessions*, Troeltsch envisions past, present, and future not as highly discrete modalities of time, related to each other in a purely consecutive manner. Instead, these three confluent dimensions interweave with, or invade, each other without sharp differentiation. Any given moment in time is a "thresholding matrix,"[11] fraught with both past and future which distend both backwards and forwards from that particular instant. In the following passage, Troeltsch compares these two rival versions of time, highlighting the most important differences which exist between them.

> This distinction eventually leads into the depths of a different *concept of time*, which underlies becoming as understood in the natural sciences and as understood in historical studies. The former is bound up with space and spatial movement, as well as with the concept of causality. The latter is bound up with inner meaning and memory that have both spatial and non-spatial contents at their disposal and place them at the service of orientation to the present and the future. The former concept of time dissects time into precisely delimited separate sections and into separate events situated within

these sections, which is possible in the final analysis only by the reduction of time to spatial occurrences. Historical time, in contrast, signifies a flow in which nothing is differentiated and isolated, but rather everything passes over into each other. Things past and things future coinhere simultaneously, every present at the same time productively bears within itself past and future, and a measurement is in general not possible, but only pauses which are inserted more or less arbitrarily in accordance with unities and great changes of meaning. [GS 3:56–57]

By inference, Troeltsch's concept of historical development also rules out two different but related views of historical becoming which had risen to prominence in the decades prior to his authorship of *Der Historismus*. These are the philosophical view of history as a progressive development and its functional equivalent in the realm of the natural sciences, the notion of evolutionary change. In the first case, the attempt to understand history in terms of the category of progress assumes "the idea of a universal, final goal to be attained by all humanity" (GS 3:57). It thus invariably posits a unilinear quality to temporal change which has a greater affinity to the natural-scientific concept of time than to real historical development. Troeltsch argues, however, that the flux of historical movement can never be channeled in one single direction. Because of the uniqueness and originality of its constituent objects, the flow of historical life can at best be analyzed in terms of a multiplicity of temporal intervals, corresponding to each entity, whose linkage to each other in terms of a universal, all-comprehensive notion of development is problematic. The concept of development appropriate to history deals only with its particular sections, and as such "is unable to trace back these entirely different, partly parallel, partly consecutive stretches [of time] to a common development. And even within every single developmental whole a number of particular lines of development cluster together to form just this whole. These lines of development in certain cases go back to a common root, or in any case finally coalesce in a unity, each, however, adhering to its own course" (GS 3:58).[12]

It was also the observation of Troeltsch and others that the concrete history of his own age disclosed a trajectory to history more like a rise and fall than a continuous ascent. There are intimations in *Der Historismus* that Troeltsch himself believed that European civilization in the decade after World War I was in a state of decline, a point of view most closely associated with Oswald Spengler.[13] However, in Troeltsch's mind such a state of affairs was finally irrelevant for the ethical task of the philosopher of history, as I will explore below.

Similarly, Troeltsch rejects a vision of history based on the category of evolution, as set forth in the natural sciences. The doctrine of evolutionary change presupposes a teleology inherent in the rise and furtherance of biological life that is as objectionable as that espoused by the philosophical doctrine of progress.

As important, however, Troeltsch's effort to distinguish historical development from temporal change as the latter is found in the natural world is not intended to deprive the process of becoming in history of any pattern and meaning. On the contrary, Troeltsch explicitly affirms the continuity that inheres in history, just as much as he denies any notion of temporality associated with rigid causal determinism. History is a fluid process, but it does not entirely lack significant configurations. Individual totalities of history are fraught with meaning and value (without which they would be indiscernible to the historian). In conjunction with their essentially dynamic nature, this fact suggests that the meaning intrinsic to any single historical object is not exhaustively disclosed without remainder at a single point in time.[14] Such meaning is instead revealed extensively (as well as intensively within the object itself) over the course of its temporal career. It exists, however obscure and prone to abrupt termination or dramatic change of direction such a career may be because of the irreducible contingency of the individual totalities of history. For Troeltsch, then, the movement of history is neither a process of inflexible chronological order nor a turbulent, utterly disorganized one. Rather, a unity of becoming permeates the historical movement among the various totalities of history that possess a unity of meaning. This allows the historian to speak of continuous and coherent interconnections or interrelationships of meaning and significance among successive phases or moments in time that are appropriate to a process of genuine development.[15] The combination of persistence and change, or mutability and duration, which thus constitutes real historical development, means that this unity of becoming is very difficult to describe logically, but seeing it and sensing it constitute the essence of historical meaning. If one speaks of this almost as a special organ of knowledge, precisely this ability is meant to understand events not by combining them in the sense of particular events with causal links, but by seeing them whole in the sense of their coalescence and fusion in a unity of becoming. (With this, of course, must also be linked a feeling for their breaking, bending, deflection, and possibly confusion.) Over against the natural-scientific concept of causality stands not merely a causal dissimilarity or individual causality in place of causal similarity, but, even more, the elevation of the causality of the particular case into a continuity of meaning, of value, or of the idea, that holds sway over the whole. [GS 3:55]

TROELTSCH'S CRITIQUE OF HEGEL'S CONCEPT OF DEVELOPMENT

Troeltsch initially presents his analysis of the concept of development in chapter 1 of *Der Historismus und seine Probleme*. This analysis, however, is supplemented in chapter 3 of this volume by an elaborate review of how this notion has been treated by an entire parade of philosophers and historians since the late eighteenth century. Under the title, "The Hegelian Dialectic," Troeltsch therein examines critically how this concept has been incorporated by the Hegelian paradigm (GS 3:243–77).

In contrast to his largely negative account of individuality in Hegel's philosophy of history, Troeltsch's investigation of the concept of historical development as it is found in Hegel discloses a fundamentally ambivalent attitude. On the one hand, Troeltsch acknowledges the importance of Hegel's notion of dialectic as a critical foundation upon which the modern idea of historical development has arisen. He affirms, once again, the impact which Hegel's thought on this subject has had upon his own understanding of history, as well as upon legions of scholars right up to the early twentieth century. "The predominance that [Hegel] gained over all the great thinkers of his own period is self-evident, as is the enormous effect on historical thought, or better yet, on the historicization of the thought of an entire generation. Indeed, this effect remains up to the present day, even with the complete disappearance of its presuppositions" (GS 3:253). On the other hand, however, Troeltsch notes that the Hegelian dialectic has its failings. Given the meta-physical assumptions to which it is intimately linked, Hegel's philosophical interpretation of history in Troeltsch's view ultimately undermines the possibility of any meaningful change occurring in history and so finally violates the concept of development as it is actually found in historical life.

Whatever its flaws, however, Troeltsch's initial perspective is that Hegel's contribution to an adequate understanding of history as a dynamic process cannot be overestimated. Hegel's notion of dialectic serves as the foundational concept upon which, for the first time, a "deep, penetrating logic" (GS 3:247) of becoming may be based. But to what in particular does this notion, in the Hegelian sense, refer? Within the framework of Hegel's epistemology, as exemplified in his *Phänomenologie des Geistes,* the idea of dialectic designates the movement of thought from a philosophically inferior position to one that is philosophically superior. This process is driven by the dynamic impulses internal to the act of thinking itself. The dialectical movement of reflection is predicated on the assumption that any given thought or concept is not a static or self-contained entity. Rather, it is inherently capable of generating or passing over to a second concept, to which it stands opposed. Similarly, the logical contradiction between the first and second concepts yields yet a third concept. This third concept subsumes that which is true in both its predecessors, in order to achieve a higher unity of thought. Guided by the same logical necessity, this process continues to generate further phases of development. It finally culminates in a moment of absolute knowledge, freed of the finite limitations, inadequacies, and obscurities of all preceding stages of cognition.

Thus, in contrast to "customary, superficial" logic, which teaches "the incomprehensibility of movement and the mutual exclusion of all antitheses," the logic of the Hegelian dialectic posits the essential identity of all such antitheses, which "flow into each other and change themselves in the movement of becoming" (GS 3:247). Summarizing the essential principles of dialectical movement,- Troeltsch writes that "it belongs to the essence of spirit not to rest, to advance from each position to its own opposite, and from here again to become aware of the unity of this opposition with the original position. This demands only this fundamental assumption concerning the essence of spirit: it is a principle of movement, of identity expressing and realizing itself only in antitheses, and the particular working-through of the logical consequences of spirit's essential nature once set in motion" (GS 3:248).

Hegel, however, did not restrict his insights regarding the notion of dialectic to the realm of human knowledge. The basic principles of dialectical logic were applied as well to history. This allowed him to construe historical life as a process of becoming whose dynamics are regulated and governed by the specific logical principles discussed above. Commenting on this feature of the Hegelian dialectic, Troeltsch asserts that "this logic of becoming and of transformation is pressed upon us nowhere so immediately as by history, in which indeed we ourselves are this becoming, and the logic of becoming is but our most characteristic self-understanding" (GS 3:248). Troeltsch also states that "as Vico had already deemed history to be the logically most penetrable part of reality, because it is our own life and product, so Hegel clearly applies to history above all this fundamental problem of becoming. He thereby penetrates his whole world picture and thinking about the world with the spirit of the dynamics evident in such logic. . . . This new logical law can be applied to the whole of human history as well as to every single part or branch selected by the historian" (GS 3:248). Indeed, in true systematic fashion, Hegel regarded all of reality as permeated with the dynamic elements characteristic of dialectical movement. "If the logic of history reveals for the first time the deepest nature of the logical, then this historical logic cannot remain confined to history, but rather must comprehend the totality of the world, even nature and the characteristic inner reality of the deity" (GS 3:248–49). Regarding an understanding of the self-movement of the divine Spirit in terms of the doctrine of dialectical motion, Troeltsch asserts that "this Spirit could only be the universal divine Spirit itself, which as fundamental activity changes eternally its dialectical and agitated essence, changes eternally from self-position as absolute activity into self-negation as given finiteness, and overcomes this eternally self-forming world-opposition in the process of world-becoming" (GS 3:250).

Hence, in Troeltsch's view, Hegel's most significant contribution to an understanding of historical becoming was to grasp the fundamentally dynamic nature of all reality and to clarify the conceptual structure of this temporal movement. Indeed, Hegelian dialectics is nothing less than "the discovery of historical dynamics" (GS 3:254).

Moreover, the logic of the movement of history elucidated by Hegel is fully consonant with Troeltsch's own understanding of historical change outlined above in this chapter. On the one hand, Hegel's dialectic, based on the identity of all antitheses and the continuous transition from one stage to another, provides the necessary element of logical unity within history by which change may be understood as fundamentally developmental. Yet, on the other hand, the fundamental dynamic principle of opposition and contradiction which underlies temporal movement guarantees that history is not a smooth sequential process. Rather, it necessarily accommodates the resistance, misdirection, and struggle characteristic of real historical development that Troeltsch insists must be maintained in any meaningful attempt to construe the processive flow of historical life. "The reality of conflicts and struggles, the contradiction of life endlessly differentiating itself, had to be taken up directly in the uniformity, continuity, and purposeful behavior of Reason, which had to give to the whole the uniformity of the principle and the law or the rhythm of becoming" (GS 3:246).

Yet, while he recognized the importance of the Hegelian notion of dialectical movement for historical thought in general, Troeltsch criticized the way in which Hegel finally interpreted the process of historical development. From the point of view of "purely historical thinking" (GS 3:273), the problem lies precisely in Hegel's linkage of the historical dialectic with the metaphysical premises which undergird his philosophy of history. This linkage reflects the same indifference to history found in his concept of the individual. The Hegelian paradigm of history assumes that the divine Spirit is the ultimate source and driving power behind the historical process. The essence of Spirit is to express or realize itself through the medium of history, according to its own inner laws, in order to attain its ultimate goal of self-knowledge. Thus, historical development is initiated by an act of self-positing on the part of the Absolute. It culminates when Spirit recognizes the production of reality in its entirety as identical to itself.

> In the first respect, Hegel makes history recognizable according to the principle that only Spirit understands itself and its production. Thus he makes humanity, history, and, in the further course of time the world in general, a production solely

of Spirit, which manifests, as well as re-establishes, its own unity in the display of antitheses. That Spirit thus understands itself in history and knows to represent its own essence, is no longer an epistemological problem. It indeed recognizes with itself its own production of the whole of reality. [GS 3:273]

According to Troeltsch, however, dialectical development from this perspective resides solely on the level of the Absolute Spirit. This thus calls into question any real temporal movement in history. By identifying change with the self-movement of the divine Reason, change at the level of the human historical world is accordingly deprived of any real significance. Any becoming at that level is understandable solely as a function of the suprahistorical development which occurs at the plane of the divine Spirit in its forward movement toward self-knowledge. Consequently, the flow of history is intelligible only insofar as it can be arranged into a rational pattern which conforms to the dialectical development in process at the level of the Absolute. This arrangement, in Troeltsch's view, is often obtained by blurring or exaggerating the differences and similarities within history. Thus, the dynamics of world history become thoroughly intellectualized, as the configuration of dialectical change intrinsic to the movement of the divine life is superimposed upon the realm of ordinary history. "Hegel attempts to rationalize the dynamics of the historical and of existence in general, to logicize history" (GS 3:273), and he is only externally or superficially concerned with the actual fluidity of historical experience.[16]

Finally, the main "philosophical objection" (GS 3:273) that Troeltsch raises regarding Hegel's notion of dialectical development is that even the dialectical movement of the divine Spirit itself involves only the semblance of change and temporal becoming, rather than real development. Hegel's own account of this process notwithstanding, the change which ostensibly occurs at the level of the Absolute, according to Troeltsch, is more apparent than real. "The logic of movement is based in a philosophy of identity, in which the 'universal Spirit' is identical with the moved expression of itself, and therefore can return to itself by means of analysis from any point of its particular realization" (GS 3:251). In Troeltsch's view, Spirit during the course of its dialectical movement may present itself in a different form by its act of self-unfolding in history. Objectively, however, it is always the same. Progressive change occurs only on the level of consciousness, not in reality, as Spirit is transformed from a state of ignorance regarding its true nature to one of true self-knowledge or self-consciousness. Thus, the movement of the divine Spirit never involves production of the new which is characteristic of real history. Instead it entails only a change in appearance, while the content of Reason remains self-identical. For this reason, then, Troeltsch argues that standing behind Hegel's dialectic of the Spirit is a doctrine of identity, or a philosophy of monism. Such a "mobilized Spinozaism" is "only an increase of consciousness, in which always the same is known, only with different fullness, clearness, and profundity. There is nothing really new and in spite of all contrasts, no creation. It is in truth only a change in form" (GS 3:275).

In sum, then, however significant may be its contribution to an adequate understanding of history, the deficiencies of the Hegelian paradigm for Troeltsch are noteworthy and tend to outweigh its benefits. In Troeltsch's view, Hegel's understanding of historical development, like his conceptualization of that which is historically individual, is incompatible with real historical experience. It involves "more and more artificiality, more and more violence" (GS 3:276). In the final analysis, the Troeltschian philosopher of history must abstract from Hegel's scheme of history its irrefutable emphasis on historical dynamics, but must foresake the metaphysical foundations by which it is secured. One must learn from Hegel the fundamental importance of the dynamic nature of historical life, without retaining the concept of the dialectical development of the Absolute that is idiosyncratic to the Hegelian paradigm. In lieu of Hegel's view of historical becoming, an understanding of "the idea of historical dynamics purely for itself" is required.

> All this has often and rightly been asserted against Hegel. But these objections refer only to the embedding of the dialectic into an epistemology and metaphysics of spiritualistic monism and to the logicization, even the scholasticization, of the dialectic following therefrom. The kernel of the latter, the idea of historical dynamics purely for itself, remains untouched. . . . There remains the possibility and necessity of organizing the dynamic flux; of comprehending nodal points of developments, the totality and rhythm of a continuity; of continually mediating the conflicts between the great primary

groups and of seeking out uniform tendencies behind all that is different and separated; finally of setting up the greatest possible connections of the whole on a planetary scale, from which everything that is individual for the first time is illuminated. [GS 3:276–77]

The Material Philosophy of History and the Crisis of Historical Relativism

I have explored above Troeltsch's understanding of the philosophical enterprise, which he names the formal logic of history. I have focused on Troeltsch's explication of the two primary categories of historical life. I have also concentrated on his efforts to distinguish the proper meaning of the historical object and historical becoming from the meaning attributed to these concepts by naturalism, and, more importantly, by the Hegelian paradigm. For Troeltsch, however, the exposition of the morphology of historical reality which he offers in *Der Historismus und seine Probleme* is the first but not the last word regarding the task of the philosophy of history. It is a necessary but insufficient condition of the satisfactory completion of this undertaking. "In truth, philosophy of history is by no means to be confined to the pure formal logic of history" (GS 3:67). By definition, the elucidation of history's formal logic is a purely contemplative endeavor. It is "a colossal achievement of the knowing intellect" (GS 3:68), whereby the essential nature of historical life is perceived and understood by the passive spectator merely for its own sake. So conceived, however, this branch of the philosophy of history is vulnerable to the label of quietism or bad historicism.[17] This is the accusation that it is nothing more than the playful, aesthetic perusal of the ongoing drama of historical life. It is a perusal conducted in a manner that is totally estranged from the urgent, even passionate, demands of real life which impinge on historians (as on all individuals) by virtue of their own personal participation and immersion in history. Accordingly, the formal analysis of history must inevitably be supplemented by an equally important moment in the philosophy of history. A material interpretation of history must be fashioned that creates a contemporary synthesis of culture. Such a synthesis is constituted by the judicious and coherent combination of values and guiding principles of life selected from the collective legacy of European civilization. Historians must eventually transcend their role as mere witnesses of historical life. Through the medium of personal decision and ethical commitment, they must actively acquire and appropriate those values and ideals from their cultural past which may be used to shape an efficacious outlook on daily life in the here and now. "Present and future must be able to attach themselves to the historical view. Wherever the possibility of such joinder does not exist, there also lacks any serious interest in history, the unity of the connection of life, from which we alone can infuse the past with the blood of a vitality that is at least historical" (GS 3:69–70).[18]

Yet, while "the logic of history passes over unawares into the material and universal construction of history" (GS 3:70), the latter presupposes the former just as necessarily as the former depends on the latter for its ultimate completion. Since "one without the other is impossible" (GS 3:70), Troeltsch also states that "construction without a logically secured empirical method is a house without a foundation, merely an ideal and sketchy product of the dreaming soul or of sovereign decree. . . . In a scientific and logical sense, the material philosophy of history must grow out of the formal. Points must emerge within the latter from which lines lead over to the former. This permits the concepts [of the material philosophy of history], at least to a certain extent, to evolve from the logic of history itself" (GS 3:70–71).

Unfortunately, Troeltsch died before he personally was able to erect a material philosophy of history upon the skeletal framework of the logical analysis of history outlined in *Der Historismus*. Nevertheless, this volume contains a glimpse, if not of the details of the cultural synthesis envisioned by Troeltsch, at least of his sense of the conditions of its possibility, as determined by his understanding of the primary categories which together constitute historical life. In particular, Troeltsch's theoretical account of historical reality heavily underscored the problem of historical relativism to which his earlier inquiries into the nature of historical values inexorably pointed. On the one hand, the category of historical development provides the conceptual framework for the continuous interconnection among past, present, and future demanded by a viable material philosophy of history. On the other hand, however, the irreducible individuality of all historical configurations of value and meaning seriously mitigates against the possibility that an enduring, universally valid value system may be established.

The concept of historical development, to which so much of Troeltsch's labor in *Der Historismus* is devoted, supplies a theoretical underpinning for any effort to articulate an effective material philosophy of history. The prerequisite of this undertaking is the individual's ability to establish vital links of connection between his own cultural past—an arsenal of available values, standards, and ideals to be drawn upon—and the standpoint in the present which he now occupies, for which such a synthesis of cultural ideals is of the utmost pragmatic import. From Troeltsch's perspective, the possibility, at least in principle, of such an enterprise is facilitated by the reality of development in history, as this idea is elaborated in *Der Historismus* as an integral dimension of the formal logic of history. Troeltsch's analysis of the category of development suggests that the dynamic quality of historical life is bound up with continuous tracts of becoming. A conceptual foundation is thus provided which allows the observer to link together the present situation and a past cultural heritage within a shared unity of becoming constitutive of the temporal movement of history. Moreover, since historical life nowhere stands still, such a synthesis must also be directed to the immediate future. For this reason, in addition to the selective retrieval of values from the past, it is imperative for the material philosophy of history to provide future direction to cultural experience. This task entails formulating cultural goals or ideal possibilities adequate to the needs of posterity, to the extent that such needs may be anticipated.[19]

> The material philosophy of history does not end here, but rather only that ends which may be worked out for it from the conditions of the formal logic of history. To put it more precisely, the summary of the present as the outcome of the entire process to date is not merely an extreme unification and deepening of one's own life-situation. At the same time, in accordance with the nature of advancing life, it is a summary for the purpose of additional formation, in which not only the past and the present, but the future as well, is postulated, and this, indeed, as act and inference based on that which presently exists. [GS 3:77]

The concept of development places the past in direct relationship to the present. It also binds reciprocally both past and present to an indeterminate future destiny that has yet to be manifested, in a temporal stream of deep continuity of meaning that is, has been, and is to come. In sum, the idea of historical development allows for the positing of a temporally unified whole necessary to perform the essential tasks of the material philosophy of history (even if such a meaningful life-process must invariably be restricted to a narrow cultural circle, rather than the entire history of humankind).

But if the notion of historical development renders theoretically feasible the construction of a cultural synthesis, the concept of individuality, as elucidated by Troeltsch in *Der Historismus*, points in the direction of an unavoidable historical relativism. As a result, it dramatically impedes any implementation of a material philosophy of history. The obverse side of Troeltsch's successful philosophical offensive to liberate historical thinking from naturalism is a heightened awareness of the originality, the contingency, the uniqueness—in short, the individuality—of all configurations of value and meaning in history. Troeltsch deeply abhorred the relativistic value-scepticism to which he feared historicism inevitably led. But his emphasis on the highly individual character of all historical phenomena illuminated the fact that values drawn from the material of history on which a present-day cultural system must be built—once regarded as absolute, eternal, and universal—are instead particular, relative, and time-bound. In a passage which echoes Troeltsch's conclusion in *Die Absolutheit des Christentums* that "the historical and the relative are identical," Troeltsch writes in *Der Historismus und seine Probleme* that the individual character of all historical totalities of meaning and value and their historically relative quality are logically correlative.

> The empirical logic of history constitutes its objects by a unity of meaning that essentially realizes itself in them, and accordingly assembles great groups of human beings and great periods of time into individual unities of meaning, for whose production the processes . . . unite . . . without realizing such a meaning absolutely and exclusively. But that means . . . that the individual meaning is always at the same time a relative value that can be beheld and felt only by a meaning that in effect bears within itself the infinite possibilities of value.

Therefore, the individual immanent value of a historical structure must first of all always be measured on its own terms, but at the same time, over and above this, it is measured in terms of a universal context of value. [GS 3:116–17]

Thus, in the final analysis, Troeltsch's sensitivity to the individuality characteristic of all historical life, and disclosed by his own exposition of the formal logic of history, ultimately demanded a renunciation of any claim to timeless, absolute standards and ideals in history. Historical thinking seemed to afford no obvious or easy escape from the relativity of all values. Such a recognition, of course, did not preclude Troeltsch from asserting that history, even in the absence of such absolutes, remains the only source for the standards that we need to construct a workable contemporary synthesis of culture. The final solution to the problems accentuated by the awareness of historical individuality is "to overcome history through history" (GS 3:772). One must cope with the problem of historical relativism by appealing to the infinite richness and abundance of concrete historical life as the living wellspring of present-day cultural and spiritual existence. Nor did Troeltsch's recourse to historically individual values and norms ever undermine his own enduring religious confidence in the reality of a divine basis to historical life. However indirectly and inchoately its presence may be intimated, the divine Reason remains as the hidden metaphysical foundation to all historical experience. Notwithstanding his critique of Hegel's view of divine involvement in history cited above, Troeltsch continued to affirm, even in the twilight of his intellectual career, that the divine depth of history must always be acknowledged in the face of the historically relative. In one of several such passages included in *Der Historismus* which echo Hegelian sentiments regarding the metaphysical basis of history, Troeltsch writes that the notion of historical development

means nothing other than such an arrangement of sequences of events and of antitheses within the few thousand years that are accessible to us. By tracing back such sequences and antitheses in the end metaphysically to an inner impulse and desire of the Reason that permeates them, and by tracing this Reason to the ultimate divine ground, to the inner movement of the divine spirit in the finite, we form an idea that lies at the frontier of all science. It is formed in very different ways according to the arrangement of those sequences. No strict science can any longer demonstrate its correctness. But it . . . forms the conclusion and ultimate background of all history. It alone guarantees us that the movement of historical-individual realities rests in an ultimate unity that only by its own agitation evades every conception and that is therefore designated only very inadequately with the words "unity" and "all." [GS 3: 173][20]

Thus, even in his final writings, Troeltsch evinces a stubborn refusal to relinquish the interpenetration of metaphysics and history which pervades his understanding of the historical process from the outset of his academic career. Accessible to faith, if not to scientific knowledge,[21] the divine Spirit is both transcendent to and immanent in history. It remains for Troeltsch the final guarantor of the meaning and value of historical life and all of its contents. "The suprahistorical surrounds history at every step and can be restrained only by a strict and always somewhat arbitrary self-limitation" (GS 3:53).

Troeltsch's Relation to Hegel in *Der Historismus*

As his last major literary work, *Der Historismus und seine Probleme* accordingly represents Troeltsch's final statement regarding the Hegelian paradigm. In this text, Troeltsch sets out to provide a systematic philosophical account of historical life that formally resembles what Hegel was attempting in his own philosophy of history, considered above in chapter 2. More than in any of his earlier writings, Troeltsch's explication of historical reality, with its accompanying critical analysis of Hegel's thought, reveals an in-depth interpretation of the nature of history that varies considerably from that of his predecessor. This dissonance between Troeltsch and Hegel is most evident in the conflict of interpretations surrounding the two foundational concepts on which Troeltsch bases his entire analysis of the formal logic of history. On the one hand, Troeltsch's acute sense of temporal realism diverges from the view of history characteristic of the Hegelian paradigm primarily in Troeltsch's unqualified affirmation of the category of individuality as definitive of historical life. Such a respect for the "reality that will not be reduced,"[22] of course, stands in marked tension with Hegel's grasp of the contingency of the historical world. The latter, at least in Troeltsch's eyes, exhibits an inadequate interest in things as they are in favor of a vision of history that disproportionately directs its sights on the realm of the suprahistorical. Similarly, Troeltsch displays equal amounts of clerkly scepticism in his disavowal of an understanding of temporal movement in terms that are totally congruent with the Hegelian dialectic. Troeltsch explicitly acknowledges the influence of Hegel concerning his own efforts to free history from total narrative anarchy. However, Troeltsch's endeavor to clarify the nature of historical becoming in *Der Historismus* stands at odds with the Hegelian version of temporal change, in ways which have been documented above.

Yet, despite the considerable disagreement between their respective visions of history, Troeltsch's philosophical interpretation of historical reality, as articulated in *Der Historismus und seine Probleme*, does not represent a total forfeiture of the use of Hegel's model of history. In the first place, Troeltsch's obvious disapproval of the notion of dialectical development and all of its metaphysical trappings should not obscure his own express appreciation of Hegel's contributions in this area. To the extent that Troeltsch recognizes and attempts philosophically to master the flux of historical becoming, his efforts reflect at least a modest appropriation of this feature of the Hegelian pattern of history. Troeltsch may finally be unable, out of respect for history as it really is, to adopt without critical challenge the full-blown version of historical development formulated by Hegel. However, his own concept of history as a developmental process fraught with continuity may be construed as at least partially indebted to Hegel, even as the Hegelian influence is greatly submerged in Troeltsch's thought. Additionally, the metaphysical turn so characteristic of Troeltsch's previous writings on the philosophy of history is detectable in *Der Historismus* as well. This is yet another instance of Troeltsch's reluctance completely to disavow this essential feature of the Hegelian paradigm. Troeltsch in this volume criticizes Hegel's philosophy of history regarding its seemingly inappropriate conjunction of the historical and the metaphysical. Nonetheless, Troeltsch himself continues to assert, in a manner thoroughly consistent with his own earlier writings, that a divine Reason permeates the historical process. This divine presence thereby undergirds the purely historical norms and values that coexist there, even if it does not absolutize any one of them.

In sum, despite his obvious deep distrust of certain elements of the Hegelian paradigm, Troeltsch's own philosophical reflection on history continued to have a real, vital relation with that of Hegel. Troeltsch's analysis of history in *Der Historismus und seine Probleme* is at times only loosely related to Hegel's philosophical vision of history. Nevertheless, the persistent influence of the paradigm in Troeltsch's own understanding of historical life, however dimly the paradigm may be perceived, suggests that Hegel's understanding of history was never wholly dispensable to Troeltsch as he tried to make sense of life as it is lived within time.

Sophisticating the Paradigm

In the preface to the third volume of his *Gesammelte Schriften,* Troeltsch describes the deep personal conflict underlying the task he had undertaken therein. His decision to concentrate on the main problems in the philosophy of history placed him in "dangerous proximity to the great authors from Voltaire and Herder to Comte and Hegel" (GS 3:vii)—giants in the history of ideas who had responsibly and creatively addressed these same problems. Yet his wariness of an encounter with these great thinkers and the unfavorable comparison which it might invite gave way to a response to the most challenging philosophical problems of his day concerning historical life. His appreciation of the seriousness of the problems themselves was sufficient motivation for Troeltsch to begin his own investigation into this subject matter, even as he drew perilously near to his predecessors. According to Troeltsch, the magnitude of these problems "is so great and sweeping that fear of competition with such great authorities ... must not frighten one away. On both the historical and the philosophical side, today's presuppositions have changed so considerably that the problems must be posed anew. The connection with those great masters nevertheless remains strong enough" (GS 3:vii).

Respect for the eminent authorities of the past, tempered by a recognition of the time's need for "a new imagining of the problems"[1] associated with historicism, in many ways serves as the leitmotiv of Troeltsch's intellectual endeavors. Indeed, Troeltsch's academic life was devoted to the effort to make sense of historical experience by way of a career-long preoccupation with the thought of one particular antecedent authority—G. W. F. Hegel. In the preceding chapters,

I have traced Troeltsch's changing relationship to Hegel, arguing that it reflects his continual attempt "to relate, by frequent alteration, an inherited paradigm to a changed sense of reality."[2]

Like Troeltsch before me, I have been lured, by virtue of the subject matter of this study, into dangerous proximity to two of the great past masters: Troeltsch himself and Hegel, by way of Troeltsch's decreation and reconstruction of Hegel's philosophy of history. My project was undertaken in response to the same mandate to pose anew the most fundamental problems of the philosophy of history. I am, of course, respectful of my predecessors' attempts to address and master, with historical depth and philosophical profundity, the problems at issue. Nonetheless, I also possess "the critic's first qualification, a scepticism, an interest in things as they are."[3] In this spirit, I conclude with a brief summary and critique of Troeltsch's critical accommodation of the Hegelian paradigm in order to illuminate the deep ambivalence lying at its core. I focus on the cluster of interrelated issues and themes which, taken together, define the shape and constitute the substance of this relationship: (1) the notion of individuality, (2) the concept of development, (3) metaphysics and history, and (4) the place of Christianity within the religious history of humanity. In these final pages, I also suggest that, with the passage of time since Troeltsch's era, what is perhaps demanded now is a more radical departure from his Hegelian lineage than even he was able to conceptualize and execute.

The Idea of Individuality

In any catalogue of his objections to Hegel's philosophy of history, Troeltsch's critique of Hegel's understanding of the notion of individuality captures his most unambiguously negative response to the Hegelian paradigm. Troeltsch's own formulations of the precise nature of that which is historically individual were shaped in equal measure by the neo-Kantian philosophical movement and the *religionsgeschichtliche Schule*. Early intimations of the latter's influence may be found in "Geschichte und Metaphysik" and *Die Absolutheit des Christentums*. But certainly by the publication of *Der Historismus und seine Probleme*, Troeltsch had borrowed and successfully assimilated the insights of both schools of thought into the nature of the historical object and was prepared to apply them, in devastating fashion, to his ongoing critical analysis of the Hegelian paradigm.

Troeltsch's lifelong antipathy toward all monistic theories of reality led him to oppose, ever more stridently, Hegel's perceived tendency to subsume what is individual in history under what is, ostensibly, ontologically more real. Thus, in both *Die Absolutheit* and *Der Historismus*, Troeltsch constructs an argument, informed by the philosophical principles of neo-Kantianism, against Hegel's attempt to identify the particular phenomena of history as the historical manifestations or embodiments of a divine essence or cause. In Troeltsch's view, any such identification only depreciates, if it does not altogether deny, the intrinsic value of the individual objects which appear in history. For Troeltsch, history abounds in surprising things. His unflagging respect for what is contingent and unique in history thereby militated against his accepting any philosophical vision of historical life (either the materialist ontology of naturalism or Hegel's equally monodimensional idealist ontology) which reduces the multifarious historical world to a single principle. In Troeltsch's view, what is truly original or individual in history must in some integral way stand apart from any underlying essence or substratum of reality, in order to preserve and protect the inviolability of its existence.

The impact of the *religionsgeschichtliche Schule* on Troeltsch further enhanced his positive valuation of the individuality of all historical events and configurations. Here individuality is construed not in terms of ontological originality but as contingency upon, or uniqueness to, a specific set of spatial and temporal variables. The insight of the modern idea of history that everything human is a product of its historical environment was deployed with special force against a central claim of the Hegelian paradigm that a particular historical phenomenon (Christianity) deserves the title of absolute religion. For Troeltsch, modern history refutes the existence of historical moments of metahistorical import. All historical entities are shaped decisively by the diverse historical factors which condition their rise and further development. This therefore prohibits equating any single one of them with the perfect or pure form of religion. None coincides with the moment of absolute self-realization on the part of the divine. From Troeltsch's historicist perspective, all objects of history are partially tainted by their temporal milieu. They must always remain as something less than perfect or absolute phenomena, regardless of the breadth or depth of their actual historical significance.

The Concept of Development

If Troeltsch is critical of Hegel's notion of individuality because of the ahistorical premises on which it is based, he is equally suspicious of Hegel's concept of development. Troeltsch often acknowledged his indebtedness to Hegel as the thinker who first established this concept on sure philosophical footing, thereby introducing it for general application by theologians and philosophers of history. Yet he repeatedly objected to the unqualified use of Hegel's interpretation of the dynamics of history in any account of historical process true to the actual nature of historical experience. According to Troeltsch, Hegel's conceptualization of historical becoming, like his notion of individuality, is anchored firmly in the metaphysical assumptions of the Hegelian paradigm and thus fails to respect our version of real time. He tentatively suggests in "Die Selbständigkeit der Religion," but argues more forcefully in *Der Historismus*, that Hegel's understanding of development in terms of the dialectical self-movement of the Absolute fixates the idea of progressive change at the level of the divine. It merely maps onto the course of human history the progress of the divine Reason toward self-realization. By construing historical development in terms of such blatantly metaphysical presuppositions, however, Hegel's view of the coherence of actual historical change finally depends upon its forced conformity to an a priori, logical framework derived from the Absolute. The Hegelian paradigm testifies to a keen sense of historical dynamics. However, retention of the intimate connection of development with the life-history of the divine, in Troeltsch's view, does indisputable violence to real history and therefore must be unequivocally rejected.

As part of his critique of the Hegelian paradigm in *Die Absolutheit des Christentums*, Troeltsch protested in other ways against Hegel's theory of historical development and his failure to comply with our imagining of temporal reality. According to Troeltsch, Hegel's concept of the procession of world history along a unilinear, evolutionary course, dictated by the dialectical self-movement of the divine, must be vehemently rejected. Troeltsch persuasively argues in *Die Absolutheit* that the empirical facts of religious history, as they are known through the methods of modern historical science, belie any arrangement of the most significant manifestations of our spiritual life along a uniform, progressive temporal course. At best, we may identify discontinuous channels of human history, each independently exhibiting developmental tendencies, without seriously entertaining the prospect of locating all of them on a single continuum of graded progress.

Finally, Troeltsch felt that Hegel's assumptions that the historical process has already ended in principle and that Christianity, as the final and perfect religion, represents the terminal point of history also contradict history as it really is. Troeltsch insists in both *Die Absolutheit* and *Der Historismus* that history is an open-ended process, extending indefinitely into the future. Consequently, no particular historical phenomenon can ever claim to be the ultimate stage of historical development. For Hegel to propound that Christianity is the absolute religion is to posit a premature ending to history. Absent a definitive conclusion to history, however, Troeltsch contends that it is impossible to survey the process of historical becoming in its entirety, or globally to evaluate its meaning. History that is still in progress precludes a totalistic historical vision. He thereby discredits one of the central claims of the Hegelian paradigm. As in other writings, Troeltsch signifies his respect for the time-bound constraints of our perspective on history in *Der Historismus*, where he renounces any world-historical overview of the meaning of history. In its place, Troeltsch commends the self-conscious limitation of the material task of philosophers of history to the particular cultural sphere to which they are confined—in his own case, that of Western European civilization.

Troeltsch was generally critical of Hegel's notion of historical development. However, his own view of history as exhibiting developmental features, and his profound obligation to Hegel for such an understanding, were factors in Troeltsch's own enterprise of sense-making throughout his career. In his earliest essays, Troeltsch employed the concept of development to exert some degree of philosophical mastery over the multiplicity of religious values found in history. By means of this concept, Troeltsch sought to discern a pattern of change and temporal succession within humankind's religious history by which this history might be regulated and ordered. More important, Troeltsch's treatment of this concept in *Der Historismus und seine Probleme* testifies to its pivotal importance in his attempt to make sense of all human history, not merely its religious dimension. As one of the twin fulcrums on which his formal logic of history was balanced, the idea of development provided Troeltsch with a crucial theoretical tool. It helped him account for the element of continuity of meaning constitutive of history amid its dynamic movement, however much he might also have acknowledged the confusion, misdirection, and contradiction embodied in our experience of temporal flux. Once detached from its metaphysical moorings, the concept of development allowed Troeltsch to discern within history certain discrete intervals of meaningful interconnection, even if such patterns might be mere fragments of the grand historical pattern envisioned by Hegel. Any such limited design, however, might be ascribed to historical movement only if it were drawn from the historical process itself. This must be done in terms of a criterion of development derived directly and inductively from within history, rather than imposed from outside history using a standard obtained by deductive philosophical methods.

Do we require a modification of our ideas about historical pattern beyond what Troeltsch himself was able to achieve? In the first place, in terms of principles intrinsic to Troeltsch's thought itself, one may question the degree to which the idea of development in history remains meaningful. Troeltsch's efforts to describe the deep structure of history rest on his analysis of its nature in terms of two discrete categories. Yet, taken to their extremes, the notions of individuality and development may not exist in a complementary relationship, and are perhaps irreconcilable. Instead they may stand in a relation of stubborn opposition to each other. To the extent that history is constituted by a spectacle of disparate individual entities, the attempt to discern pattern and meaning among such entities is problematic, if not impossible. If all that emerges in history, as Troeltsch insists, is truly novel, unique, and heterogeneous, then the dynamic interconnections among historical objects are reduced to the status of perpetual transition, devoid of any properties of orderly or coherent succession. Conversely, to the degree that history may be characterized in developmental terms, the imposition of such a formal pattern upon the contingent realities of history threatens to consume its individual moments under a quasi-narrative rubric. The notion of development implies continuity among its interconnected parts. Continuity in turn suggests a minimum of commonality among historical moments, which may negate the novelty or utter difference characteristic of their very being.

Troeltsch's tentative resolution to the dissonance that exists in history between the form embodied by developmental change and the fact of an utterly contingent world appears in his last essays. These writings disclose the culmination of a seemingly inexorable movement in a direction favoring the latter as the predominant category of historical life. In "The Place of Christianity among the World Religions," Troeltsch notes his increasing obsession during the course of his career with the conception of radical individuality. It is a "conception which dominates the whole sphere of history" and whose significance "impresses me more forcibly every day."[4]

> History cannot be regarded as a process in which a universal and everywhere similar principle is confined and obscured. Nor is it a continual mixing and remixing of elemental psychical powers, which indicate a general trend of things towards a rational end or goal of evolution. It is rather an immeasurable, incomparable profusion of always-new, unique, and hence individual tendencies, welling up from undiscovered depths, and coming to light in each case in unsuspected places and under different circumstances. Each process works itself out in its own way, bringing ever-new series of unique transformations in its train, until its powers are exhausted, or until it enters as component material into some new combination.[5]

If what is individual is given primacy as a category of history's formal logic, however, the viability of development as an interpretive device descriptive of historical experience is proportionally diminished. As a result, the narrative order implied by development is itself subjugated to history's nonsequential contingencies. With the affirmation of the brute contingency of modern reality, historical change becomes merely a series of discontinuous, isolated moments, destitute of any significant links and connections of affinity. Moreover, Troeltsch's own sense of the open-endedness of the historical process points to an ineradicable awareness of time as purely successive or disorganized. Since we live in an unfinished world, our attempt to find patterns of any kind in historical time becomes acutely difficult. In the absence of a final end, history loses its elementary plot-like features and seems nothing more than the meaningless flux and flow of events. Without the form that an end implies, time as we moderns perceive it within our common experience consists of an endless, and so a shapeless, world. Any effort to discern or impose order or pattern on such a labyrinthine temporal flow must consequently be recognized as an activity that is at best ineffectual and, at worst, illusory.

Metaphysics and History

One of the crucial elements of Troeltsch's critical retrieval of Hegel was his appeal to an Absolute reality for the ultimate legitimation of the relative values of history. Troeltsch was increasingly adamant throughout his career in acknowledging "the relativity and transitoriness of all things, even . . . the loftiest values of civilization."[6] Troeltsch never failed, however, to rescue the values of history from religious or ethical nihilism by positing the reality of a metaphysical dimension within history, to which the relativities of history are somehow intimately related and of which they partake. For Troeltsch, the historical process is the medium of God's self-revelation or communication, apprehensible only via faith. It is characterized by the intimate commingling of divinity and humanity.

In keeping with his understanding of historical development as incomplete, Troeltsch (in contrast to Hegel) denies to history the full and unconditional manifestation of the Absolute. Instead, he relocates this manifestation to a moment which, for now, lies beyond the present. In Troeltsch's theological interpretation of history, God becomes linked with the power of the future. It is imminent to, rather than immanent within, history. Thus, the concept of the still-to-come end of the historical process acquires a deep metaphysical richness. Nevertheless, despite this modification of the Hegelian paradigm, Troeltsch's confidence throughout his academic career in the reality of a divine dimension to history was undying. From the coda of "Geschichte und Metaphysik" that "only the metaphysical—

and never the historical—brings salvation"[7] to the closing words of "The Place of Christianity among the World Religions" that "to apprehend the One in the Many constitutes the special character of love,"[8] Troeltsch discloses his own lasting preference for the metaphysical interpretation of history associated with Hegel.

Yet Troeltsch's attempt in this way to avoid the uninhibited relativism that he (and others) dreaded endangers the intellectual coherence of his program to address the problem of historical relativism. One of the great strengths of this program is its unabashed and honest acknowledgment of the historicity and finitude of everything human. The assertion of a metaphysical element as the ultimate guarantor of normative certainty and objective religious truth thereby represents a move beyond the self-imposed limits of Troeltsch's historicist perspective and signifies a fundamental failure of clerkly scepticism on his part. Unfortunately, his propensity to solve the problem of historical relativism on nonhistorical grounds ultimately suggests a subtle denial of history and thereby begs more questions than he is able to resolve.[9]

Toward the end of his career, an intimation of Troeltsch's own wariness on this score appeared in his reminder in *Der Historismus und seine Probleme* that one may attribute only mythic status to the concept of the Absolute. "The Christian doctrine of the self-disclosure of an actively moved divine Spirit in the finite is a myth. It has led, however, to the finest and deepest psychological observations, which lay bare the mysteries of the soul much more deeply than cool psycho-genetic or aprioristic theories were able to do" (GS 3:213). Without disparaging the pragmatic power of myths as models to live by, I find this brief but noteworthy hint of Troeltsch's own sense of the fictiveness of the Absolute to be significant. It seems inevitably to move him beyond any reliance upon fictions in his attempt responsibly to live in time and change. Troeltsch thereby avoids the regression into the paradigm that is otherwise so tangible in his writings.

The Place of Christianity in Religious History

Finally, despite his sustained criticism in *Die Absolutheit* of Hegel's contention that Christianity represents the final, perfect, and absolute religion, Troeltsch's own apologetic endeavors leave no doubt that for him Christianity occupies a central, even perhaps an unparalleled, place within world religious history. Troeltsch's last word on this subject, in one of his posthumously published lectures intended for delivery in England, reveals a quite moderate position regarding the truth of Christianity in relation to other religions. The recognition of Christianity as "in some degree, a manifestation of the Divine Life itself," whose validity for Western civilization is "final and unconditional," "does not preclude the possibility that other racial groups, living under different cultural conditions, may experience their contact with the Divine Life in quite a different way, and ... may quite sincerely regard this as absolutely valid for them, and give expression to this absolute validity according to the demands of their own religious feeling."[10] Yet a vestige of Hegel's understanding of the unique historical status of the Christian religion undeniably persists in Troeltsch's previous writings which deal with this subject. Troeltsch recognizes "how thoroughly individual is historical Christianity after all, and how invariably its various phases and denominations have been due to varying circumstances and conditions of life."[11] Yet Troeltsch regards Christianity, if not as a truly absolute religion, at least as firmly ensconced in a distinctive place in the history of religions separate from other religious traditions. For all his stated reservations against this notion—misgivings which became more explicit as his career progressed—Troeltsch occasionally asserts that history is not without its quasi-evolutionary tendencies. Within this modified Hegelian view of historical development as a process leading to a single goal, Christianity, alone among the positive world religions, "occupies a unique position which signifies an essentially new level of development" (AC 121). It has "the distinctive task to make itself the crystallization point for the highest and best that has been discovered in the human spiritual world" (AC 127). Troeltsch's reluctance to deny that Christianity may yet be surpassed with the advance of time is offset by his equal unwillingness (at least in *Die Absolutheit*) to abdicate the claim that Christianity represents the pinnacle of religious development, thereby possessing at least a kind of absoluteness. At yet another point, then, Troeltsch rejoins the Hegelian paradigm, at that particular place where his apologetic instincts and convictions at least temporarily hold sway over his critical acumen.

In sum, Troeltsch's critical response to Hegel's philosophical interpretation of history in large part involves his incredulous reaction to many of its main features. His own vision of history compelled Troeltsch, often with considerable urgency, to highlight what to him were serious flaws and deficiencies in Hegel's understanding of historical experience, as he sought to make more adequate sense of life as it is lived within time. As a result of Troeltsch's critical scrutiny of Hegel's thought, the Hegelian paradigm of history gives way to other, more successful attempts at sense-making. To borrow Frank Kermode's observation in *The Sense of an Ending*, with Troeltsch, "we may look back at these historical patterns with envy, but without any sense that they can ever again be useful, except as fictions patiently explained" (27).

But Troeltsch's critical response to Hegel's thought also entails an appropriation of many of its central features, a selective borrowing that coexists with his sceptical rejection of other elements. "Time will always reveal some congruence with a paradigm," notes Kermode (129), and the case of Troeltsch's relation to Hegel is no exception: "The paradigms do survive, somehow," and their survival "is as much our business as their erosion" (43). And, indeed, Troeltsch's effort to make sense of historical experience in the shadow of Hegel discloses the continuing presence of the paradigm at various loci where Troeltsch found it necessary and convenient for his own use.

Thus, notwithstanding his keen sense of historical realism and his frequent attempts to abandon the Hegelian paradigm in its name, Troeltsch's efforts were not entirely successful. Though often qualified and denied, the paradigm remained a permanent feature of Troeltsch's thought. Troeltsch's relation to Hegel includes an element of subordination to the paradigmatic fictions, even if, at times, these fictions are inconsistently and hesitatingly related to his own efforts at sense making. And so, "we re-create the horizons we have abolished, the structures that have collapsed; and we do so in terms of the old patterns, adapting them to our new worlds" (Kermode 58).

Nevertheless, whatever critical failings we may identify in Troeltsch's labors "to speak in terms of a modern reality . . . without forfeiting the use of the paradigm" (106), the significance of his endeavors remains unquestionable. Indeed, "what interests us is, very often, the effort itself" (106). Despite its flaws, Troeltsch's attempt to make sense of historical life by way of a systematic and penetrating consideration of the Hegelian paradigm, gives voice to the necessary struggle to break free of the paradigms by virtue of an engagement with reality. It also articulates the inevitable recognition that all such fictions, "though prone to absurdity, are necessary to life" (155). In our world, the material for sense-making has perhaps become "more elusive, harder to handle" (31) than before, although the past has left us with satisfactory resources in this endeavor. Such materials now include the thought of Troeltsch and Hegel and what may be gleaned from the relation of one to the other. Both remain among the thinkers to whom we, as well as our successors, will turn to consider the degree to which we moderns, situated and entangled in the here and now, attended to "the relations between fiction and reality" (152).

Notes

Chapter 1: Troeltsch, Hegel, and the Changing Fiction

1. Kermode, *The Sense of an Ending*, 7.

2. I borrow these phrases from H. Ganse Little's analysis of the structure of temporality in *Decision and Responsibility*.

3. Unsigned review of Kermode, *The Sense of an Ending*, in *The Economist*, 8 July 1967, 125.

4. Throughout his book Kermode employs the central term *fiction* as both a descriptive and a value-laden category. In the first place, this term primarily denotes any imaginative structure which attempts to organize our temporal experience along the lines of a narrative—that is, a story with a clearly defined beginning, middle, and end. When used in this manner, the notion of fiction may include (as Kermode notes) the theological plot enclosed in the Bible and (as I argue in the following pages) Hegel's secular philosophy of universal history. The term *fiction* may also designate fictitious literature (e.g., novels) and any construct invented by the imagination (e.g., fictions of the end, the fiction of the Absolute). The latter may be labeled subsidiary fictions, insofar as they often stand in an auxiliary relationship to fictions in their primary sense. (For example, the apocalyptic fiction of the end is a component part of the larger fiction that the Bible contains.)

Beyond its merely descriptive aspect, however, the term *fiction* also implies the fictive status of these entities and so suggests a judgment as to their correspondence to real existence. Indeed, for Kermode, all fictions are by their nature projections of "the desires of the mind on to reality" (*The Sense of an Ending*, 42). They can make no claim to objective truth. Instead we must assess them in terms of their ability to help us "make sense of and to move in the world" (37). In Kermode's view, this ontological status of all fictions remains constant, "however conscious some, as against others, may become of the fictive quality of these fictions" (44).

For a discussion of Kermode as a representative of "the conservative fictionalist tradition in modern poetics and philosophy," see Lentricchia, *After the New Criticism*, esp. 31–39. See also Ricoeur, *Time and Narrative*.

5. For an alternative view which insists upon the intrinsic narrativity of temporal life, see Crites, "The Narrative Quality of Experience."

6. "According to Bergson," Maurice Natanson writes in his Introduction to volume 1 of the *Collected Papers* of Alfred Schutz, "a true philosopher says only one thing in his lifetime, because he enjoys but one point of contact with the real. Understood in its proper sense, this means that whatever variegation and richness a philosophical mind may possess, however extensive its interests and research, there is ultimately but one cardinal insight into reality that it achieves, one decisive illumination on which everything else turns and which is the philosopher's claim to truth." See Alfred Schutz, *The Problem of Social Reality*, vol. 1 of *Collected Papers*, ed. Maurice Natanson (The Hague: Martinus Nijhoff, 1962), xxv. For Troeltsch, it may be said unequivocally that his status as a true philosopher is guaranteed by the way in which the effort to deal with the problems of the historical world was the pivot upon which all of his intellectual labors turned.

7. This phrase is Kermode's and is introduced on p. 10 of *The Sense of an Ending*.

8. Troeltsch, *Christian Thought*, 6.

9. Within this last category, see, for example, Arthur C. Danto, *Analytic Philosophy of History* (New York: Cambridge University Press, 1965); A. Donagan and B. Donagan, *Philosophy of History* (New York: Macmillan, 1965); William H. Dray, *Philosophy of History* (Englewood Cliffs, N.J.: Prentice-Hall, 1964); and W. H. Walsh, *Philosophy of History: An Introduction* (New York: Harper, 1960).

10. Kermode, *The Sense of an Ending*, 41. Kermode borrowed this phrase from Wallace Stevens, who in turn borrowed it from Hans Vaihinger. See Vaihinger, *The Philosophy of 'As If': A System of the Theoretical, Practical and Religious Fictions of Mankind*, trans. C. K. Ogden (London: Routledge & Kegan Paul, 1924), 77; and *The Collected Poems of Wallace Stevens* (New York: Vintage Books, 1982), 404.

11. Unfortunately, the text of Hegel's lectures on the philosophy of history is notoriously problematic. Like other lecture series by Hegel (and one by Troeltsch) which were published posthumously, this text is actually a composite of material taken from two different sources: Hegel's own manuscript material and a collation of notes from various student auditors of Hegel's course in this subject. Although I have in fact borrowed freely from both texts within the text, the second-hand material cannot share precisely the same degree of authenticity which the verbatim passages penned by Hegel himself possess. In addition, various versions of

Hegel's lectures on the subject of the philosophy of history may be found in both German and English which are more or less reputable in the eyes of Hegel critics. In keeping with scholarly consensus in this matter, all passages in this study will be taken from Hegel's *Lectures on the Philosophy of World History* (hereafter cited as LPH). This corresponds to the preferred German edition of Johannes Hoffmeister [*Vorlesungen über die Philosophie der Weltgeschichte. Erste Hälfte: Die Vernunft in der Geschichte* (Hamburg: Felix Meiner, 1955)].

To complicate matters further, the Nisbet/Hoffmeister text does not represent the entirety of Hegel's philosophical reflections on history, but instead constitutes only volume 1 of his lectures. Hegel's introduction to the basic principles of his interpretation of history is followed by a three-part companion text which contains his extended philosophical commentary on the actual history of the world. Citations from the latter are taken from J. Sibree's English translation of Hegel's *Vorlesungen über die Philosophie der Geschichte*, ed. Theodor Litt (Stuttgart: Philippe Reclam, 1961)—an edition prepared by Hegel's son, Karl. See Hegel's *The Philosophy of History* (hereafter cited as PH).

12. One might say that the medium is indeed the message in the case of Troeltsch. The process nature of his thought is detailed in his autobiographical essay, "Meine Bücher" (1922), found in his *Gesammelte Schriften* (hereafter cited as GS).

13. For a relatively recent and expansive bibliography of Troeltsch's writings, see Friedrich Graf and Harmut Ruddies, eds., *Ernst Troeltsch Bibliographie* (Tübingen: J. C. B. Mohr, 1982). This compilation has now displaced the list of Troeltsch's works prepared by Hans Baron and found in GS 4:863–72.

14. See Hans-Georg Drescher's comment in "Ernst Troeltsch's Intellectual Development" that Troeltsch's procedure in *Der Historismus und seine Probleme* is informed by his "characteristic linking of historical review with a systematic perspective." In John P. Clayton, ed., *Ernst Troeltsch and the Future of Theology*, 28.

15. Troeltsch, "Die christliche Weltanschauung und ihre Gegenströmungen," GS 2:227–327; "Wesen der Religion und der Religionswissenschaft," GS 2:452–99; "Die Selbständigkeit der Religion," *Zeitschrift für Theologie und Kirche* 5 (1895): 361–436; 6 (1896): 71–110, 167–218 (hereafter cited as SR); and "Geschichte und Metaphysik," *Zeitschrift für Theologie und Kirche* 8 (1898): 1–69.

16. Troeltsch, *The Absoluteness of Christianity and the History of Religions* (hereafter cited as AC).

17. Published in 1922 as the third volume of Troeltsch's *Gesammelte Schriften*.

18. Troeltsch, *Protestantism and Progress*, 18.

19. For a defense of the thesis that the philosophical enterprise as carried out by any great philosopher (especially including Hegel) is "a kind of poetry," see Quentin Lauer, "Hegel as Poet," in Robert L. Perkins, ed., *History and System: Hegel's Philosophy of History*, 1–14.

20. For a listing of the secondary literature on Troeltsch through 1975, see Clayton, *Ernst Troeltsch*, 200–214. Also useful, especially regarding more recent publications, is the bibliographical essay by Trutz Rendtorff and Friedrich Graf which follows their contribution on Troeltsch in Smart, Clayton, Katz, and Sherry, eds., *Nineteenth Century Religious Thought in the West*, 3:305–32, esp. 328–32.

In light of the range and specificity of the secondary work on Troeltsch, it remains surprising that his relationship to Hegel, where it is discussed at all, is usually mentioned only aphoristically or has received, at best, only superficial treatment or passing attention. See, for example, the pithy statement by James Luther Adams that "of Troeltsch it may be said that he . . . historicized Hegel," in "Ernst Troeltsch as an Analyst of Religion," *Journal for the Scientific Study of Religion* 1 (October 1961): 109. An instance of the latter tendency is found in Rupp, *Christologies and Cultures*. Rupp devotes a brief section of his chapter on the relationship between Christology and non-Christian religions to a consideration of the significance of the Troeltsch-Hegel connection for his study ("Hegel, Troeltsch, and Religious Pluralism," 226–29). The brevity of Rupp's treatment of Hegel and Troeltsch together, as well as its subordination to an analysis of larger issues, exemplifies the manner and extent to which the relationship between these two thinkers generally has been considered within the secondary literature.

An important recent work in which the author places at the center of his own constructive theological reflection on history a consideration of Hegel, revised in part by Troeltschian insights, is Hodgson, *God in History*.

21. See, for example, O'Brien, *Hegel on Reason and History;* Dunning, *The Tongues of Men;* and the compilation of essays found in the volume edited by Perkins cited above.

22. Alasdair MacIntyre, ed., *Hegel: A Collection of Critical Essays* (Garden City, N.Y.: Doubleday, 1972), 219.

Chapter 2: The Hegelian Paradigm

1. Although here he discusses traditional historiography as a monolithic entity, this category is actually an internally differentiated whole, as Hegel makes clear in the 1822 and 1828 drafts of his lectures. He indicates in these

drafts that there are in fact two different types of historical studies in contrast to philosophical history: "original" history and "reflective" history (which is itself further subdivided into "universal," "pragmatic," "critical," and "specialized" history). For Hegel's enumeration and critical description of the distinguishing features of these various modes of historical writing, see LPH, 11–24.

2. Hegel's terminology with regard to the ultimate principle of the cosmos is infamously diverse. He variously designates this principle as Reason, the Idea, the Absolute, and the World Spirit (or simply "Spirit"). In the course of this essay, I will assume that a fundamental homogeneity of meaning exists among these terms. Reference to this entity will follow Hegel's own usage in the passage under consideration at any given time, with the caveat that this usage varies widely throughout the text of his lectures.

3. For the sake of clarity, I will express the distinction between reason as a cognitive process and Reason as a metaphysical reality by capitalizing the word when it refers to the latter and not the former.

4. Additional evidence is interspersed throughout Hegel's lectures which reinforces his view of the divine status of the Idea, as well as the inherent duality of transcendence versus immanence within his concept of God. See, for example, Hegel's positive description of the Idea as "true, eternal, and omnipotent" (LPH 28); his statement that the universal object of the philosophy of history is that which is "infinitely concrete, all-comprehending and omnipresent" (LPH 31); and its characterization as self-identical—"the spirit is eternally present to itself; it has no past, and remains for ever the same in all its vigour and strength" (ibid.).

For a thorough examination of Hegel's doctrine of God, see Lauer, *Hegel's Concept of God.*

5. Hegel's effort to reinterpret the religious doctrine of providence in philosophical terms is, of course, merely one instance of his general propensity to translate virtually all of the major doctrines or symbols of traditional Christianity (e.g., the Incarnation and the Trinity) into the ostensibly more adequate conceptual language of philosophy. For a critique of Hegel's systematic attempt to reconcile Christian faith and speculative philosophy in this way, which takes as its point of departure Hegel's interpretation of history, see Dunning's comparative study of Hegel and J. G. Hamann cited in chapter 1.

6. As noted above, Hegel is a firm believer in, and spirited advocate of, our capacities as thinking beings. He thus adamantly affirms the human rational consciousness, rather than ostensibly subrational or unreflecting modes of knowledge such as feeling or emotion, as the highest, and, indeed, the only appropriate form of cognition for members of the human species. "When God reveals himself to man, he reveals himself essentially through man's rational faculties; if he revealed himself essentially through

the emotions, this would imply that he regarded man as no better than the animals, who do not possess the power of reflection—yet we do not attribute religion to the animals. In fact, man only possesses religion because he is not an animal but a thinking being. It is a trivial common-place that man is distinguished from the animals by his ability to think, yet this is something which is often forgotten" (LPH 39).

7. According to Hegel, Spirit's knowledge of itself in the external world is never direct, but is always mediated by our finite consciousness, to which it is intimately related. Generally speaking, the World Spirit's self-knowledge is grounded in the consciousness of the particular nation-state prominent at any given time during the course of world history. "The Spirit's own consciousness must realise itself in the world; the material or soil in which it is realised is none other than the general conscious-ness, the consciousness of the nation" (LPH 52). But, more specifically, the World Spirit manifests itself in the consciousness of human individ-uals, who are the primary vehicles of the Spirit's knowledge of itself. From Hegel's perspective, this claim is justifiable for several reasons. First, as an omnipresent reality, the divine Spirit is in fact "present in everyone and appears in everyone's consciousness" (LPH 52–53). As important, just as the world-at-large is an instantiation of the cosmic Spirit, so too are all finite creatures incarnations of the divine Reason, sharing, in a sense, in the reality of God. "The relationship of men to [the World Spirit] is that of single parts to the whole which is their sub-stance" (LPH 52). Thus, by postulating such a close relationship between the infinite Spirit and all finite spirits, Hegel can in his own terms reason-ably argue that the former can only come to a true knowledge of itself via the medium of the latter's consciousness. For Hegel's account of the devel-opment of absolute knowledge from the point of view of finite spirit, see his *Phenomenology of Spirit*.

8. In addition to defining the goal of world history primarily in terms of Spirit's arrival at self-knowledge, Hegel also identifies the purpose of world history in terms of its ultimate attainment of freedom, which (as is the case with self-consciousness) Hegel associates with its substance or essence: "freedom is the substance of Spirit," he says; "the Spirit is by nature self-sufficient or free" (LPH 47). If one may understand the course of world his-tory in cognitive terms as a triphasic movement from a state of precon-sciousness (Reason before it posits the world), through a state of consciousness (Reason aware of the world as an object other than itself), to a final state of self-consciousness (Reason aware of the world as identical to itself), one may view the same process in volitional terms as well. From the latter perspective, the passage of world history follows a pattern whose phases are structurally similar to the former, but in which the goal is defined in terms of Reason's growing powers of self-determination. In this

light, Reason passes from a phase of unrelatedness (Reason prior to the existence of the world), through a phase of dependency (Reason in relation to an external point of reference, i.e., a world that is ostensibly different from itself), to a final state of self-dependency or freedom (Reason in relation to a world which it recognizes as identical to itself). In the final analysis, however, this difference in terminology only obscures the essential homogeneity of meaning between the two notions in question. For, as Hegel asserts, "freedom, by definition, is self-knowledge" (LPH 55), or "Spirit, in its consciousness of itself, is free" (LPH 53).

Moreover, just as the World Spirit's attainment of self-knowledge is mediated by our subjective consciousness, so are human spirits the primary organs of its eventual realization of freedom. The course of world history, when seen from below, may be described as "the progress of the consciousness of [human] freedom" (LPH 54). As such, it parallels the Spirit's progressive realization of freedom as discerned from above. More specifically, the gradual recognition of human freedom occurs in discrete stages over the course of world history. These are the recognition (1) that *"one* is free" (the ruling despot) in the Oriental world, (2) that *"some* are free" (the governing aristocracy) in the Greco-Roman world, and (3) that *"all* men as such are free" in the Germanic-Christian world (ibid.). These different degrees of the knowledge of freedom on the part of the human spirit coincide with the three major divisions of Hegel's analysis of world history. For a more extended discussion of these periods, see below, "Hegel's Material Philosophy of History."

9. The reader already familiar with the thought of Troeltsch will notice that some of the categories employed here (for example, the formal logic and the material philosophy of history) are borrowed directly from Troeltsch's writings on the philosophy of history. While I remain faithful to the organizational structure of Hegel's own lectures, my use of this terminology at the same time anticipates important connections between Hegel and Troeltsch on this subject. It thereby serves as a helpful heuristic device within the overall framework of this study.

10. The correlative doctrines of the cunning of Reason and the function of human activity as the means at times insidiously employed by the divine Reason to serve its ends both raise and resolve, at least in Hegel's mind, the ever-vexing issue of theodicy. For Hegel, the tragic fate of individuals in history is only one instance of the many negative aspects of existence which confront the observer of world history. "We cannot fail to notice how all that is finest and noblest in the history of the world is immolated upon its altar" (LPH 43). Nonetheless, despite the enormity of the misfortune and human wreckage which may be found there, the pathos of history is more tolerable if one appreciates the affirmative side of this process as well. When one recognizes that Reason must necessarily employ the agents of history in its fashion in order to serve its own higher or divine purposes, it

is possible to contemplate the fact of evil in the world from a more cosmic perspective than might otherwise be available. From this elevated point of view, one may accept the negative consequences which seem inevitably to befall humanity in history as a humble price to pay for the realization of the ultimate design of the world. Indeed, from this angle of vision, it may even be feasible vicariously to share the seeming callous indifference of Reason, which itself "cannot stop to consider the injuries sustained by single individuals, for particular ends are submerged in the universal end" (ibid.). In the final analysis, then, one may become reconciled to the harsh reality of evil and negativity in the world by adjusting one's perspective on this matter. Once this has been done, any distress over the negative results of history may be counterbalanced by an appreciation of the positive role which they play, so that ultimately the negative may be "reduced to a subordinate position and transcended altogether" (ibid.).

11. In this regard, see Hegel, *Hegel's Philosophy of Right*.

12. For Hegel, the interrelationships among art, religion, and philosophy—the similarities and differences which unite and separate these modes of human knowledge—are a highly significant feature of his own philosophical analysis of the ideational component of human culture. In Hegel's view, these three modalities share access to the truth, and, hence, are essentially similar in content. They are, however, distinguishable with regard to the form by which this truth is represented, along the following lines. In art, the truth is presented in terms of tangible works of beauty which appeal to, and are derived from, the realm of the senses. "The aim of art is to make the divine immediately perceptible and to present it to the imagination or intuition" (LPH 105). Religion, on the other hand, employs symbolic forms, such that the truth is present to human powers of representation. Finally, philosophy makes use of the medium of conceptual thought. Hegel places these modalities along a continuum which ranges from less to more adequate expressions of the truth, culminating in the philosophical form—one which "in its own way, is the highest, freest, and wisest of the three" (ibid.). For a more comprehensive treatment of these basic modes of human apprehension, see Hegel's lecture series on each of these three topics.

13. Hegel's account of the development of religion places great emphasis upon the diverse conceptions of God or the Absolute which emerge in its course. This emphasis is reinforced by his extended discussion of religion in the *Phenomenology*. It is hardly true, however, that Hegel reduces human religiosity to its intellectual dimension. For Hegel, religion is an affair of the heart and the will as much as it is a matter for theological speculation. True religion must therefore integrate into a unified whole piety, moral rectitude, and ratiocination. For Hegel's appreciation of the nonintellectual sides of religious life, see especially his essays on religion from his Tübingen years, as collected in his *Early Theological Writings*.

14. In addition to the internal reasons cited above, there is an important extrinsic justification for this choice. In his critical appropriation of the Hegelian paradigm, Troeltsch relied heavily on Hegel's philosophical interpretation of the history of the world religions, especially Hegel's contention that Christianity represented the apex of this history, and so deserved the title of the absolute religion. The different ways in which Troeltsch both accepted and rejected Hegel's philosophy of the history of religions will be discussed at greater length in chapters 3 and 4.

15. Hegel, *Lectures on the Philosophy of Religion* (hereafter cited as LPR).

16. As Hegel indicates, the religions of China in different ways possess quasi-theistic features which point to a concept of ultimate reality consonant with that typical of religions at this stage in the development of the religious consciousness (for example, the notion of *T'ien*, or the concept of *Tao*). But, as Hegel also correctly asserts, religion in Chinese culture is more a matter of moralism or ethics (as the centrality of the teachings of Confucius in Chinese civilization suggests) or of state-religion (as indicated by the importance of emperor-worship) than one of metaphysical or theological speculation. Hence, it is a less exemplary instance of this category of religion than, for example, the Vedic tradition in India. With regard to the other great religious tradition of India—Buddhism—Hegel notes that, despite its essentially atheistic character, it too may be seen as a religion of nature. The Buddhist affirmation of nonbeing or nothingness as the ultimate reality, and the Buddhist quest for the annihilation of all particularity, qualify it as a monistic view of the universe and so as a religion which reduces all reality to a single principle. The "fundamental dogma" of Buddhism is that "Nothingness is the principle of all things—that all proceeded from and returns to Nothingness . . . for in themselves all things are one and the same inseparable essence, and this essence is Nothingness" (PH 168–69). Finally, the other religions of the Oriental world which Hegel considers—Zoroastrianism and the religions of Syria and Egypt—mark the transition between nature religion and the next phase of the evolution of the religious consciousness. For example, the Zoroastrian religion contains certain intimations of an emergent dualism, with its postulation of the antithesis between Good and Evil (as personified in the figures of Ormazd and Ahriman). Nevertheless, in the religion of Persia, the divine is expressed in naturalistic terms as the power of Light. Thus, it is still constrained by the limitations of nature, rather than perceived as an entity totally separate and distinct from the natural world.

17. Within the triumvirate of the religions of spiritual individuality, Roman religion is the third element. In Hegel's view, the religion of Rome shares common features with both Greek and Jewish religion. The polytheism of Roman religion is strikingly similar to that of the religion of Greece, but, in the former, the gods are co-opted to the service of the Roman state. Indeed, it is the state itself which is ultimately divinized in the religion of

Rome, and which acquires a universal status and omnipotence that closely resembles the God of Judaism. As a result, the religion of the Roman empire is unable to transcend the mundane qualities of a universal state religion. Consequently, it is seen by Hegel as ultimately a spiritual dead end which, as such, heralds the arrival of Christianity.

18. Hegel's assessment of Christianity as part of his mature philosophical reflection is undoubtedly quite positive. However, his appreciation of the Christian religion changed considerably during the course of his intellectual career. For his earlier, more critical, evaluation of the Christian faith, see his *Early Theological Writings* cited above.

Chapter 3: The Crisis of Religion in the Modern World

1. Quoted in Köhler, *Ernst Troeltsch*, 1.

2. For a brief examination of the way Troeltsch's "writings as a whole are a veritable microcosm of this turn-of-the-century intellectual turmoil," see Rubanowice, *Crisis in Consciousness*, 1–16.

3. For an alternative analysis by Troeltsch of the nature and cause of this disunion, see his Die wissenschaftliche Lage und ihre Anforderungen an die Theologie.

4. Significant by its omission from this group, of course, is the modern idea of history. Troeltsch's analysis of the effects of historical thinking on Western religious and cultural values is found primarily in texts written later in his career. I will consider these works in chapters 4 and 5.

5. See also the statement of Hampson, in *The Enlightenment*, that "science . . . seemed to have dispensed with the need for God as a necessary factor in its explanation of the universe" (91).

6. As Troeltsch implies, this synthetic vision of the underlying unity of the cosmos has been elaborated in the rigorous systematic form appropriately employed by technical philosophy and grasped more intuitively and immediately by the artistic and poetic *Gestaltungskraft* characteristic of neohumanism and embodied in the latter's gospel of beauty. Perceived from the latter, aesthetic point of view, "the unity of being is the unity of spirit and nature in the work of art; the unity of becoming is the unity of poetry's capacity for beauty . . . unfolding itself in a lawful manner" (GS 2:233).

7. In addition to the radical challenge which it posed to the dualistic cosmology of traditional Christianity, the immanent-aesthetic ethic espoused by neo-humanism presented an alternative to the traditional Christian view of morality. According to the Christian dualism "of this-worldliness and other-worldliness" (GS 2:234), the moral agent attains an ultimate state of supernal bliss by obeying a set of heteronomous dictates proposed by a supernatural lawgiver. In contrast, the neohumanist perspective envisioned

our moral activity exclusively as a present-worldly phenomenon of self-development. According to this perspective, "the individual is harmoniously to unfold from within himself his given capacity and riches in serene, certain, and clear joyousness of life" (GS 2:233).

8. H. B. Acton writes that theism "is the view that God has created a world beyond or outside himself so that the material world, though dependent upon him, is not an aspect or appearance of him." *The Encyclopedia of Philosophy*, s.v. "Idealism."

9. All citations are from the English translation, "Religion and the Science of Religion," in *Ernst Troeltsch: Writings on Theology and Religion*, ed. and trans. Robert Morgan and Michael Pye (Atlanta: John Knox Press, 1977), 82–103 (hereafter cited as RSR).

10. As Troeltsch notes further, this classic opposition between idealism and positivism is one with deep roots in the history of Western ideas. It is nothing less than "the age-old opposition between Platonism and realist empiricism, although each in its own way has now assimilated the modern concept of nature. In more modern terms it is the contrast between Kant and Hume, and to relate it even more to the present, it is the contrast between the positivism of the Comte and Spencer school against the interpretation of mind offered by Hegel and those akin to him" (RSR 82–83). For an alternative account by Troeltsch of this dichotomy within the field of the study of religion, see also his essay dedicated to the memory of William James and entitled "Empiricism and Platonism in the Philosophy of Religion."

11. Troeltsch stresses that the idealism of which he speaks does not impugn the reality of the material world. It merely highlights the power of mind repeatedly to bring forth the diverse manifestations of human culture. For this reason, he clearly allies himself with the camp of metaphysical or objective idealism, which opposes both the reduction of mind to material reality and the doctrine of the "mere phenomenality" (RSR 83) of the physical world, and not with the antirealist presuppositions of subjective idealism. For a discussion of the distinction between these types of idealist thought, see *The Encyclopedia of Philosophy*, s.v. "Idealism."

12. The emphasis upon the differences between these undertakings, however, should not conceal the important relationship between them. According to Troeltsch, the proper execution of the task of psychological analysis is assumed by epistemology as its necessary point of departure. "The psychology of religion is the basis and presupposition of all epistemological investigations. The phenomenon has to be seen in its factuality and in its objective individuality before we can ask about its validity" (RSR 114).

13. See, especially, "Zur Frage des religiösen Apriori," GS 2: 754–68.

14. Troeltsch's appreciation of the sociological dimension of religion is reflected primarily in *Die Soziallehren der christlichen Kirchen und Gruppen*

(*The Social Teachings of the Christian Churches*), originally published in 1912 as the first volume of his *Gesammelte Schriften*. Troeltsch's historical analysis of Christian social doctrine in this text technically falls outside of the formal enterprise of the science of religion. However, its methodological spirit is consistent with the task of the scientific study of religion considered in this chapter. *Die Soziallehren* is informed by the thesis that a relationship of mutual reciprocity holds between Christianity in any of its sociological forms and the sociocultural, political, and economic structures with which it interacts. Troeltsch is thus able to affirm the autonomy of religion as a social phenomenon, even as he acknowledges that the realm of religion is also subject to influence and modification at the hands of the so-called real forces of the world.

15. The relationship between historical research and what may be designated as the philosophy of the history of religions is based on the transition from descriptive analysis to critical adjudication. It is thus formally parallel to the link between the psychology of religion and epistemology, described above as part of the turn to the subject within the science of religion.

16. Troeltsch, "Geschichte und Metaphysik," 52, n.1.

17. Ibid., 43.

Chapter 4: Historical Relativism and the Crisis of Religious Values

1. In Troeltsch's career, *Die Absolutheit* occupies a logical (if not, strictly speaking, a chronological) intermediate point within his vast literary output. It forms "the conclusion of a series of earlier studies [discussed in chapter 3] and the beginning of new investigations of a more comprehensive kind in the philosophy of history"—namely, his later, more systematic philosophical reflections on history contained in *Der Historismus und seine Probleme* (Troeltsch, *Christian Thought*, 4).

In part, as he indicates in an early footnote to this text, the transitional nature of *Die Absolutheit* resides in Troeltsch's turn therein toward the southwest German neo-Kantians—Wilhelm Windelband and especially Heinrich Rickert—with a concomitant lessening of the impact of Hegel on his thinking. He writes that "the strongly Hegelian standpoint that appeared [in "Geschichte und Metaphysik"] has here been transformed into a critical one, due to the influence of Rickert" (AC 168, n.4). As Troeltsch rightfully acknowledges, Rickert's quest to establish universally valid values epistemologically rather than by means of ontological speculation concerning history—with its strikingly anti-Hegelian overtones—remained influential on Troeltsch's own philosophical consideration of history. It bore fruit almost immediately in an essay entitled "Moderne Geschichtsphilosophie" [GS 2:673–728] and, later and more extensively, in *Der Historismus und seine Probleme*.

It is beyond the scope of this study to examine at length Troeltsch's relation to his predecessors and contemporaries other than Hegel. In the present chapter and in chapter 4, however, I recognize (but do not elaborate upon) the bearing of neo-Kantianism upon Troeltsch's analysis of the historical object and the kind of causality operative in history as a major impetus to Troeltsch's critique of Hegel's thought. Nevertheless, even as his head is tilted toward the neo-Kantian brand of philosophy, Troeltsch never appropriated fully all of its philosophical doctrines, rejecting especially its decidedly antimetaphysical orientation. With Hegel, Troeltsch consistently stood by a fundamentally metaphysical interpretation of history throughout his entire career, a feature of his philosophy of history upon which this essay focuses considerable attention. Thus, notwithstanding his leanings away from the Hegelian paradigm as evinced by his captivation with Rickert and Rickert's philosophical colleagues, Troeltsch remained bound to certain foundational claims of Hegel's philosophy of history. These bonds will be discussed at greater length in this and the following chapter.

2. For Troeltsch's more elaborate discussion of the rise of historical thinking, see the following essays "in which I have thrown some light on the historical development of the modern approach to history" (AC 167, n.1): "Ueber historische und dogmatische Methode in der Theologie" [GS 2:729–53]; and "Aufklärung," "Deutscher Idealismus," and "Deismus" [GS 4:338–73, 429–87, 532–86].

3. In principle, the crisis of historical relativism confronts all religious worldviews in which at least a modicum of historical consciousness has appeared. In practice, however, Troeltsch restricts his analysis to the impact which historical thinking has had on the Christian tradition, in part because of the emergence there of various apologetic strategies over the centuries which attempt self-consciously to deal with this problem. He also does so, in part, because of his own personal commitment to the Christian heritage and his desire to defend it in the face of this crisis.

4. In the fields of historical research into early Christianity and its major documents, enormous gains have come from applying the tools of modern historical interpretation to the Christian religion and the events upon which it is based. But the relevance of secular historical thinking to questions of faith and history in general, and the viability of Troeltsch's specific formulation of the historical method in particular, have hardly been uncontroversial in twentieth-century theological circles. Indeed, the attempt to rescue, or at least to establish on more sure footing, the validity of the historical convictions of Christianity in the face of the apparent threat posed by secular historical understanding has been a focal point of the work of many important theologians since Troeltsch's era. These include even those, such as Wolfhart Pannenberg, who otherwise are in sympathy with Troeltsch's project. For a brief discussion of the stages

which this debate has taken after Troeltsch, see Dunning, *The Tongues of Man*, 7–26. The classic discussion of the faith/history debate in contemporary theology, which also takes Troeltsch's three-pronged historical method as its springboard, remains that of Van Harvey in *The Historian and the Believer: The Morality of Historical Knowledge and Christian Belief* (New York: Macmillan, 1966).

5. Although this apologetic strategy is most closely associated with the philosophical reflection of G. W. F. Hegel, it does have other precursors and progenitors in the history of Western thought. These include Johann Gottfried Herder, Immanuel Kant, and Gotthold Ephraim Lessing, whose philosophies of history may all be seen as anticipations of the full-fledged evolutionary model of history propounded by Hegel. Of special note is Friedrich Schleiermacher, whose own apologia for the Christian religion relied heavily upon a developmental account of the history of religions.

6. Troeltsch perceptively notes that while Christianity in the Hegelian scheme is indeed "the highest and final stage of religion," it too must be superseded, in a sense, by a philosophical version of its essential truths, as the philosopher translates the Christian religious symbols into rational concepts. Christianity was for Hegel "merely the last of the preparatory stages that, though remaining limited to symbols, would lead to the absolute religion. This absolute religion was to evolve out of Christianity as a purely mental construct" (AC 77).

7. Troeltsch sets forth a more extensive analysis of the category of individuality as it applies to historical life in *Der Historismus und seine Probleme*. I discuss this analysis at greater length in chapter 4.

8. For Troeltsch, the absence of certitude about the end of history renders the notion of an absolute religion theoretically impracticable. It also serves retroactively to cast doubt both upon the nature of the universal principle which generates the historical process in the first place and upon all intermediate stages. It thus throws into total confusion all speculation about the entirety of history. "But if that is how matters stand, how can the universal principle be characterized with sufficient certainty as long as its definitive realization still lies far off in the incalculable distance? And if the character of the universal principle cannot be determined with certainty, how then can its stages be described with certainty—those stages by which it has moved toward realization up to the present time and among which we are supposed to make a choice?" (AC 69).

9. In this regard, Troeltsch endorses the conclusions of his radical theological predecessor, D. F. Strauss. Strauss's life's work was in many ways dedicated to the notion (in opposition both to Hegel and Schleiermacher) that history is not an appropriate arena for absolutes of any kind. For Troeltsch's brief summary of Strauss's critique of Hegel and Schleiermacher, see AC 78.

10. Troeltsch's use of the terms *individuality* and *uniqueness* to characterize all historical phenomena is a nuanced one. His argument against reducing all historical events and occurrences to natural variables was designed to protect the fundamental ontological originality of such phenomena, rather than to interpret them as mere epiphenomenal by-products of the basic structures of nature. In the present context, however, the individuality of any given historical phenomenon is seen more as a function of the particular spatial and temporal conditions from which it arises. By virtue of their unrepeatability, these conditions confer a uniqueness upon the historical creations which emerge out of them.

11. The issue of the further development of Christianity raises in turn the question of whether, and to what extent, the later history of the Christian religion and its concrete individual forms may be understood and interpreted in terms of a specific controlling principle or underlying essence. For Troeltsch's analysis of this particular issue, see "Was heisst 'Wesen des Christentums'?" (GS 2:386–451). In this essay Troeltsch enters into conversation with various other theologians (Harnack, Loisy, F. C. Baur, et al.) who have explored this issue.

12. The criterion for the evaluation of the historical religions is by no means free-floating. It is instead implanted firmly in a specific religious tradition. According to Troeltsch, "we cannot regard the criterion as an entity that hangs in midair above the historical religions but as something that requires us to choose among them in a process of free development. The criterion will emerge from the religion that is strongest and most profound, appropriating from the others only what has been worked out with particular effectiveness. It must be rooted in a positive, historical religion" (AC 96).

In addition, Troeltsch's insistence that the criterion be one which arises empirically from actual historical data directly rebuts the means used by Hegel in the evolutionary apologetic theory discussed in the previous section of this chapter. As Troeltsch notes both here and in earlier essays considered in chapter 3, the norm employed within the Hegelian paradigm to evaluate the stages of development in the evolution of religious history is not one that emerges inductively from history itself. Rather, it is the product of an a priori notion of God and so is applied deductively to world history. The truth of Christianity from this perspective "could be demonstrated only by drawing inferences from the absolute principle inhering in the absolute idea that works itself out in history. Accordingly, the idea of the absolute religion was taken not from history but from the concept of the absolute itself. The concept of the absolute was regarded as a rationally necessary concept of God, but it appeared in history only as an end product of thought" (AC 77).

13. As Troeltsch recognizes, the act of personal decision by which we choose a particular value system from among the diversity of such systems

available to us is itself conditioned by the temporal moment in which the choice is made, just as the value orientation which is adopted is so conditioned. For an analysis of the hermeneutical dynamics intrinsic to this process which is especially sensitive to the historicity of both the subjective and objective poles of interpretation, see Hans-Georg Gadamer, *Truth and Method,* trans. G. Barden and J. Cumming (New York: Seabury Press, 1975).

14. In addition to asserting the superiority of Christianity over the Indian religions of Hinduism and Buddhism, Troeltsch affirms his preference for the Christian religion versus the so-called religions of law—Judaism and Islam—which represent the failure to overcome various particularistic and idiosyncratic restraints. According to Troeltsch, the concept of God in the Jewish and Islamic religions has not been sufficiently disengaged from "the natural confinement . . . to state, blood, and soil" (AC 109) to rival the universalism of the Christian deity. They therefore must be seen as fundamentally deficient.

15. In terms of the notion of salvation, the religions of law designated above are inferior to Christianity, according to Troeltsch, because in them redemption "remains forever bound to achievements that man produces out of his own nature" (AC 110) or by virtue of "his own strength" (AC 114). They thereby fail totally to dissever the natural sphere and the world of higher, transcendent values celebrated by Christianity.

Chapter 5: Historical Relativism and the Crisis of Cultural Values

1. While in *Die Absolutheit des Christentums* he restricts his focus exclusively to the impact of this problem on the world of religious values, Troeltsch expands its scope in *Der Historismus* to include "the relation of individual historical facts to standards of value within the entire domain of history in connection with the development of political, social, ethical, aesthetic, and scientific ideas" (Troeltsch, *Christian Thought* 23). The latter work is intended to answer the question of "how one may discover the way from the historically relative to valid cultural values." Thus, "it is the old problem of the Absolute in a much broader perspective, and taken up with orientation to cultural values as a whole, and not merely to the religious position" (GS 4:14). Stated in different terms, the relationship between *Die Absolutheit* and *Der Historismus* is like that of two concentric circles to each other. Both share a common center (an overriding concern with the problem of historical relativism), but have radii of different length (the variable breadth of the historical horizon within which this common problem is addressed). They thus encompass areas of greater or lesser magni-

tude.

2. As he noted in his preface to *Der Historismus*, Troeltsch self-consciously chose to renounce "the more aristocratic monological style of many of my colleagues." He decided instead to shape his studies in this work "in continuous discussion with those who have written on similar themes" (GS 3:viii).

3. Hegel is one of the seminal thinkers in the philosophy of history whose contributions are selected for special treatment and consideration in *Der Historismus*. Two sharply demarcated subsections of the work are devoted solely to Hegel's thought on the most pertinent categories of the philosophy of history that Troeltsch identifies. My decision to attend to Troeltsch's critical analysis of Hegel's philosophy of history was made in order to keep in sharp focus the main thrust of my essay. However, it risks ignoring his insightful reflections on a multitude of other significant thinkers, in relation to whom Troeltsch formulated his own ideas on the nature of history. In order to rectify, in part, this willful omission, I refer the reader to Robert J. Rubanowice, "Ernst Troeltsch's History of the Philosophy of History," *History of Philosophy* 14 (1976). In this essay may be found a concise but cogent summary of Troeltsch's "own critical account of the history of the philosophy of history" (81) from Greek thought to Troeltsch's own day.

4. For an excellent analysis of German historiography in and around the time of Troeltsch's career, which includes a discussion of Troeltsch's own contribution to this field, see also Iggers, *The German Conception of History*, esp. 174–95.

5. In Troeltsch's view, however, insofar as both naturalism and historicism share a common philosophical root, the adversarial relationship that exists between these two dominant positions is best understood, in some ways, as a sibling rivalry. For his brief analysis of how both of these tendencies derive from the Cartesian analysis of consciousness that precipitates modern philosophical reflection in general, see GS 3:104ff.

6. The shared intent of Dilthey and Rickert to differentiate between *Naturwissenschaften* and *Geisteswissenschaften* should not obscure the significant distinctions between them regarding precisely what accounts for these dissimilar modes of knowledge. Dilthey locates the difference in the objects under examination. Rickert, on the other hand, finds it in the distinctive methodological approaches (the idiographic in contrast to the nomothetic) employed by the subject.

7. See GS 3:31 for Troeltsch's apparent willingness to side with Dilthey on this issue. His entire methodological approach in *Der Historismus*, of course, gives eloquent testimony to this preference.

8. Troeltsch makes this argument briefly but trenchantly in the second

chapter of *Der Historismus und seine Probleme*. See, especially, GS 3:130–33.

9. See, e.g., GS 3:245, where Troeltsch acknowledges Hegel's appreciation for that which is "original, animate, individual, and contrary" in history.

10. Troeltsch's notion that the historical interconnection among objects encompasses increasingly greater intervals of history ultimately points, in principle, to a notion of universal history—a concept, however, which Troeltsch rejects in actual practice. For a discussion of Troeltsch's ambivalence towards the extendability of the scope of historical development to the entire history of humankind, see below, note 12.

11. This phrase is borrowed from Little, *Decision and Responsibility*, 2.

12. As indicated above in note 10, however, a genuine tension may be found in Troeltsch's thought in *Der Historismus* between the pragmatic necessity of delimiting the range of historical development to the temporal interval enclosed by the lifetime of the particular objects of history and the theoretical possibility of widening the scope of historical becoming to include the greatest imaginable horizons—namely, the history of humankind in its entirety, or universal history. On the one hand, Troeltsch's sensitivity to the dynamic and interactive qualities of the various individual totalities found in history compels him to entertain the notion that, at its farthest reaches, the developmental process may be extended to the outer limits (both past and future) of human history.

> At first . . . interesting becoming takes place purely within the historical object as its own development, far remote from us. Such becoming, however, never takes place in isolation, but always in interaction with other totalities, and it is precisely from their cross-fertilizations and combinations that the richest and most important formations arise. . . . But this already requires us to locate the development of a particular totality in the mutual collision and movement of contiguous totalities. There is not one single history of development. But if that is not possible, each of the more deeply penetrating descriptions must always embrace the intertwining of different totalities and thereby finally widen the circle to the farthest limit: all of humanity (72).

Yet, on the other hand, Troeltsch clearly acknowledges the logical difficulties which meet every attempt—including that of Hegel—to envision and attempt to interpret the history of the whole of humankind. The notion of the development of humanity

> appears not only as a superhuman achievement, exceeding every possibility of knowledge and acting sometimes as idle and vigorous,

sometimes as fanciful and mythical. It appears also as logically impossible, since the entirety of human development does not at all lie before us, and thus cannot at all be interpreted. Hegel was right to affirm this completedness, when he wished to interpret history, but he was, of course, wrong in that he wanted to interpret it at all. Some day there may perhaps be a unity of humankind as a result of definite historical processes and contacts, and then such an interpretation may be possible, provided that one can master the mass of events in tradition and memory to an extent sufficient for such a purpose. But this is not yet the case, and, consequently, such a philosophy of history is in fact utterly impossible. [GS 3:74–75]

In the final analysis, Troeltsch himself accedes to the practical limitations imposed upon the philosopher of history noted above. He restricts the scope of historical development accessible to observation and eventual interpretation to the particular cultural circle in which he and his contemporaries found themselves. This was the theater of European civilization. For a further discussion of this issue in *Der Historismus*, see pp. 173–74, 188–89, and 703–30.

13. Oswald Spengler, *The Decline of the West*, 2 vols., trans. C. F. Atkinson (New York: A. A. Knopf, 1945).

14. That the meaning embodied in any given individual totality of history is neither readily nor entirely available at any single point in time is implied by the category of the unconscious which Troeltsch appends to the primary concept of individuality. According to this notion, "our actions, feelings, instincts, aspirations, and decisions bear in themselves many more assumptions than we know and have a much greater or quite different significance for the whole and for the long run than we ourselves were conscious of" (GS 3:47). Because of this fact of historical life, however, the meaning of any given historical configuration is never available or accessible at any single moment—especially not its point of origin. It only gradually becomes clear over time, and is only fully penetrable retrospectively, once its lifetime has expired. Troeltsch's category of the unconscious thereby bears a striking resemblance to Hegel's notion of the cunning of reason. Both emphasize the long-term ramifications of historical actions of which the performer is initially ignorant. For Troeltsch, however, the significance of these actions and events remains on the plane of the historical, while for Hegel, of course, a cosmic intentionality is presupposed that goes beyond mere history.

15. See also Little's statement that "development exists only insofar as a common meaning or cultural spirit underlies it or is formed in the flowing of events. When this happens, a unique concrete connection of becoming occurs which is distinguished by movement toward a common cultural

result." Little, "Ernst Troeltsch and the Scope of Historicism," 355.

16. Despite his accusation that Hegel failed adequately to appreciate the developmental quality of real history, Troeltsch took pains to exonerate him from the charge of a prioristic constructionism, for which he has often been derided. Hegel may have attempted to construe historical change in terms of an ahistorical schema. It was Troeltsch's belief, however, that Hegel never attempted to deduce the actual data of history in an a priori fashion. Instead, he worked inductively with the empirical material available from critical historical investigation as the starting point for his analysis of the pattern of temporal becoming to be found there.

> Hegel . . . by no means proposes to eliminate investigation which proceeds empirically and critically, pragmatically and psychologically. He rather presupposes them, and only later arranges their materials according to the principle of the dialectic, whereby we might wish that investigation and preparation themselves be anointed with a drop of dialectical oil. The dialectical picture of history is the reconstruction of given, evident, and concrete materials into a whole, not the aprioristic deduction of what occurs with regard to its content and the sequence of events from the Idea. This is extremely important, and unfortunately has often been endlessly mistaken or misunderstood. [GS 3:253–54]

17. According to Troeltsch, "This is the . . . second aspect of the charge against historicism, which is felt almost more strongly today than the first [i.e., the naturalistic view of history]. This sort of thing, however, is [equally] intolerable" (GS 3:69).

18. Indeed, Troeltsch challenges the possibility that any scientific enterprise can exist in the form of unadulterated reflection, utterly divorced from its practical implications or implementation:

> There is no purely contemplative science, neither in nature nor in history, neither in motive nor result. Spinoza's pure contemplation flowed into ethics. Kant's pure theory sought to rise above knowledge in order to make room for faith. Pure natural science bears its fruits for spiritual mastery over the perplexing fullness of reality and for technological needs. Both serve as its motive as well as its outcome. Therefore, there is also no purely contemplative history that does not flow into understanding of the present and of the future. [GS 3:70]

19. Troeltsch's formulation of the task of the material philosophy of history as involving both a retrospective and a prospective moment highlights an additional grievance which he files against the Hegelian paradigm. This griev-

ance concerns what Troeltsch designates as the problem of the future for Hegel. It is a fundamental tenet of Hegel's philosophy of history that the final goal of history, if not the actual termination of all historical events, has already been attained in the Germanic-Christian civilization of Hegel's own day. Thus, for Hegel, the substantive interpretation of history is purely a retrospective task, for which any future historical developments have no intrinsic bearing. In Troeltsch's view, however, the genuine open-endedness of human history demands that consideration be given to the future as well as the past, in the manner briefly indicated above. For Troeltsch's critique of Hegel on this issue in *Der Historismus*, see 131–32 and 254–55.

20. See also, for example, Troeltsch's statement that "The formation of the criteria and especially the synthesis of the criteria . . . are therefore a matter of faith in the deep and full sense of the word: the contemplation of a content formed from life as expression and revelation of the divine ground of life and of the inner movement of this ground toward a total meaning of the world—a meaning unknown to us—the grasping of the ideal of culture that proceeds from the given situation as a representation of the unknowable Absolute" (GS 3:175).

21. As Troeltsch emphasizes, the philosophy of history requires "a subsidy of faith in a divine Idea revealing itself in the given" (GS 3:692).

22. Kermode, *The Sense of an Ending*, 106.

Chapter 6: Sophisticating the Paradigm

1. Kermode, *The Sense of an Ending*, 80.
2. Ibid., 128.
3. Ibid., 64.
4. Troeltsch, *Christian Thought*, 13–14.
5. Ibid., 22.
6. Ibid., 7.
7. Troeltsch, "Geschichte und Metaphysik," 69.
8. Troeltsch, *Christian Thought*, 35.
9. This conclusion is shared by Thomas W. Ogletree, who writes in his comparative study of Troeltsch and Karl Barth that "the most striking thing about Troeltsch's viewpoint is that he has found it necessary to turn away from the concreteness and individuality of history in order to avoid the skeptical conclusion to which his approach to history pushes him. Consequently, the category of history in spite of its manifest importance to Troeltsch is not in the last analysis sufficient to legitimate religious and moral values in human life and culture. In order to attain that end Troeltsch must rather look

to a nonhistorical dimension in human experience." See Ogletree, *Christian Faith and History*. Cf. Reist, *Toward a Theology of Involvement*, 84–87.

10. Troeltsch, *Christian Thought*, 26–27.

11. Ibid., 22.

Selected Bibliography

Works by Ernst Troeltsch

The Absoluteness of Christianity and the History of Religions. Translated by David Reid. Introduction by James Luther Adams. Richmond: John Knox Press, 1971.

Christian Thought: Its History and Application. London: University of London Press, 1923.

"Empiricism and Platonism in the Philosophy of Religion." *Harvard Theological Review* 5 (October 1912): 401–22.

Gesammelte Schriften. 4 vols. Aalen: Scientia, 1961–66.

"Geschichte und Metaphysik." *Zeitschrift für Theologie und Kirche* 8 (1898): 1–69.

Protestantism and Progress: A Historical Study of the Relation of Protestantism to the Modern World. Translated by W. Montgomery. Foreword by B. A. Gerrish. Philadelphia: Fortress Press, 1986.

"Religion and the Science of Religion." In *Ernst Troeltsch: Writings on Theology and Religion.* Translated and edited by Robert Morgan and Michael Pye, pp. 82–103. Atlanta: John Knox Press, 1977.

"Die Selbständigkeit der Religion." *Zeitschrift für Theologie und Kirche* 5 (1895): 361–436; 6 (1896): 71–110, 167–218.

Die wissenschaftliche Lage und ihre Anforderungen an die Theologie. Tübingen: J. C. B. Mohr (Paul Siebeck), 1900.

Works by G. W. F. Hegel

Early Theological Writings. Translated by T. M. Knox. Chicago: University of Chicago Press, 1948.

Hegel's Philosophy of Right. Translated by T. M. Knox. Oxford: Oxford University Press, 1967.

Lectures on the Philosophy of Religion. Translated by P. C. Hodgson, et al. Berkeley & Los Angeles: University of California Press, 1988.

Lectures on the Philosophy of Religion. 3 vols. Translated by Rev. E. B. Speirs and J. Burdon Sanderson. New York: Humanities Press, 1962.

Lectures on the Philosophy of World History. Translated from the German edition of Johannes Hoffmeister by H. B. Nisbet. Introduction by Duncan Forbes. Cambridge: Cambridge University Press, 1975.

Phenomenology of Spirit. Translated by A. V. Miller. Foreword by J. N. Findlay. Oxford: Oxford University Press, 1977.

The Philosophy of History. Translated by J. Sibree. Introduction by C. J. Friedrich. New York: Dover Publications, 1956.

Secondary Sources

Bodenstein, Walter. *Neige des Historismus: Ernst Troeltschs Entwicklungsgang.* Gerd Mohn: Gütersloh, 1959.

Clayton, John Powell, ed. *Ernst Troeltsch and the Future of Theology.* Cambridge: Cambridge University Press, 1976.

Collingwood, R. G. *The Idea of History.* Oxford: Oxford University Press, 1969.

Crites, Stephen. "The Narrative Quality of Experience." *Journal of the American Academy of Religion* 39 (1971): 291–311.

Dunning, Stephen N. *The Tongues of Men: Hegel and Hamann on Religious Language and History.* American Academy of Religion Dissertation Series, no. 27. Missoula, Mont.: Scholars Press, 1979.

Dyson, A. O. "History in the Philosophy and Theology of Ernst Troeltsch." Ph.D. dissertation, Oxford University, 1968.

Edwards, Paul, gen. ed. *The Encyclopedia of Philosophy.* 8 vols. New York: Macmillan/Free Press, 1972.

Engell, James. *The Creative Imagination: Enlightenment to Romanticism.* Cambridge, Mass. & London: Harvard University Press, 1981.

Fackenheim, Emil L. *The Religious Dimension in Hegel's Thought.* Chicago: University of Chicago Press, 1967.

Findlay, J. N. *Hegel: A Re-examination.* New York: Oxford University Press, 1976.

Gilkey, Langdon. *Reaping the Whirlwind: A Christian Interpretation of History.* New York: Seabury Press, 1976.

Hampson, Norman. *The Enlightenment.* New York: Penguin Books, 1976.

Hodgson, Peter C. *God in History: Shapes of Freedom.* Nashville, Tenn.: Abingdon Press, 1989.

Iggers, Georg G. *The German Conception of History: The National Tradition of Historical Thought from Herder to the Present.* Middletown, Conn.: Wesleyan University Press, 1968.

Kermode, Frank. *The Sense of an Ending: Studies in the Theory of Fiction.* New York: Oxford University Press, 1967.

Köhler, Walter. *Ernst Troeltsch.* Tübingen: J. C. B. Mohr (Paul Siebeck), 1941.

Lakeland, Paul. *The Politics of Salvation: The Hegelian Idea of the State.* Albany: State University of New York Press, 1984.

Lauer, Quentin. *Hegel's Concept of God.* Albany: State University of New York Press, 1982.

Lentricchia, Frank. *After the New Criticism.* Chicago: University of Chicago Press, 1980.

Lessing, Eckhard. *Die Geschichtsphilosophie Ernst Troeltschs.* Theologische Forschung, vol. 39. Hamburg-Bergstedt: Herbert Reich, 1965.

Little, H. Ganse, Jr. *Decision and Responsibility: A Wrinkle in Time.* AAR Studies in Religion, no. 8. Tallahassee, Fla.: American Academy of Religion and Scholars Press, 1974.

———. "Ernst Troeltsch and the Scope of Historicism." *Journal of Religion* 46 (1966): 343–64.

Löwith, Karl. *Meaning in History.* Chicago: Phoenix Books, 1958.

O'Brien, George Dennis. *Hegel on Reason and History: A Contemporary Interpretation.* Chicago & London: University of Chicago Press, 1975.

Ogletree, Thomas W. *Christian Faith and History: A Critical Comparison of Ernst Troeltsch and Karl Barth.* New York & Nashville, Tenn.: Abingdon Press, 1965.

Perkins, Robert L., ed. *History and System: Hegel's Philosophy of History.* Proceedings of the 1982 Sessions of the Hegel Society of America. Albany: State University of New York Press, 1984.

Reardon, Bernard M. G. *Hegel's Philosophy of Religion.* New York: Barnes & Noble, 1977.

———. *Religion in the Age of Romanticism: Studies in Early Nineteenth Century Thought.* Cambridge: Cambridge University Press, 1985.

Reist, Benjamin A. *Toward a Theology of Involvement: The Thought of Ernst Troeltsch.* Philadelphia: Westminster Press, 1966.

Ricoeur, Paul. *Time and Narrative.* 3 vols. Translated by Kathleen McLaughlin and David Pellauer. Chicago & London: University of Chicago Press, 1984–88.

Rubanowice, Robert J. *Crisis in Consciousness: The Thought of Ernst Troeltsch.* Foreword by James Luther Adams. Tallahassee: University Presses of Florida, 1982.

———. "Ernst Troeltsch's History of the Philosophy of History." *History of Philosophy* 13 (1976): 79–95.

Rupp, George. *Christologies and Cultures: Toward a Typology of Religious Worldviews.* The Hague: Mouton, 1974.

Smart, Ninian, John Clayton, Steven Katz, and Patrick Sherry, eds. *Nineteenth Century Religious Thought in the West.* 3 vols. Cambridge: Cambridge University Press, 1985.

Taylor, Charles. *Hegel.* Cambridge: Cambridge University Press, 1977.

Taylor, Mark C. *Journeys to Selfhood: Hegel and Kierkegaard.* Berkeley & Los Angeles: University of California Press, 1980.

Walzel, Oskar. *German Romanticism.* Translated by A. E. Lussky. New York: Frederick Ungar, 1965.

Welch, Claude. *Protestant Thought in the Nineteenth Century.* 2 vols. Vol. 1, 1799–1870; Vol. 2, 1870–1914. New Haven & London: Yale University Press, 1972–85.

White, Hayden. *Metahistory: The Historical Imagination in Nineteenth-Century Europe.* Baltimore: Johns Hopkins University Press, 1978.

Wilkins, Burleigh Taylor. *Hegel's Philosophy of History.* Ithaca & London: Cornell University Press, 1974.

Williamson, Raymond Keith. *Introduction to Hegel's Philosophy of Religion.* Albany: State University of New York Press, 1984.

Wyman, Walter E., Jr. *The Concept of* Glaubenslehre: *Ernst Troeltsch and the Theological Heritage of Schleiermacher.* American Academy of Religion Academy Series, no. 44. Chico, Calif.: Scholars Press, 1983.

Yasukata, Toshimasa. *Ernst Troeltsch: Systematic Theologian of Radical Historicality.* American Academy of Religion Academy Series, no. 55. Atlanta: Scholars Press, 1986.

Yerkes, James. *The Christology of Hegel.* American Academy of Religion Dissertation Series, no. 23. Missoula, Mont.: Scholars Press, 1978.

Index

Absolute, the: fiction of, 151n.4; Hegel and, 8–12, 71–73, 75, 77, 101, 105, 106, 117, 119–20, 128–30, 142, 155n.2 (*see also* God, Hegel and; Reason, Hegel and; Theology, evolutionary theory of); Troeltsch and, 12, 15, 101–3, 105, 147, 166n.1 (*see also* God, Troeltsch and). *See also* Absoluteness, religious: Christianity and

Absoluteness, religious: Christianity and, 79, 80–93, 100–101, 106, 165–66n.12; questioning of, 80; Troeltsch vs., 92–95, 164n.8

Absolutheit des Christentums und die Religionsgeschichte, Die (Troeltsch), 14; and *Der Historismus und seine Probleme* contrasted, 166–67n.1; Hegel criticized in, 79–107

Abstract, and concrete contrasted, 40

Acton, H. B., 161n.8

Adams, James Luther, 154n.20

Agnosticism, Hegel vs., 25

Ahriman, 159n.16

Alexander the Great, 32

Anaxagoras, 24

Animal(s): man as, 60; and man contrasted, 156n.6

Anthropology, Christianity and, 55

Anthropomorphism, in Greek religion, 45–46

Apologetics, Christian, 80–94, 99, 100. *See also* Orthodoxy, supernatural theory of Christian; Theology, evolutionary theory of

Aristocracy, Greco-Roman: freedom and, 157n.8

Art: neohumanism and, 57, 160n.6; religion, philosophy, and, 158n.12

Astronomy: history and, 4; revolutionary developments in, 54

Atomism, 55

Aufhehung, 39

Augustine, Saint, 122

Awe, religious, 66

Baron, Hans, 153n.13

Barth, Karl, 171n.9

Baur, F. C., 165n.11

Beauty, neohumanist concept of, 57–58

Becoming: Hegel on, 126–27, 129–30, 137, 170n.16 (*see also* Development, historical: Hegel on); unity of, 125, 133. *See also* Development, historical

Bergson, Henri, 152n.6

Bible: as "fiction," 151n.4; miracles in, 81

Biology, history and, 4

Bliss, religious, 66

Brahman, 43, 44, 45

Buddhism, 96; and Christianity contrasted, 99, 166n.14; Hegel on, 42, 159n.16

Caesar, Julius, 31, 32

Categorical imperative, 61

Causality, 21, 115. *See also* Universal causality

Chance, as history element, 116

About the Author

George J. Yamin, Jr., is an assistant regional attorney for the U.S. Department of Health and Human Services. *In the Absence of Fantasia: Troeltsch's Relation to Hegel* is his first book.

Yamin received his B.A. in religion from Williams College, his Ph.D. in Christian theology from the University of Chicago Divinity School, and his J.D. from the Northwestern University School of Law. His present scholarly interests, in addition to modern religious thought, include the intersection of theology, health care ethics, and law in the areas of right-to-die litigation and the AIDS crisis.

Yamin and his wife, Margaret, reside in Chicago, Illinois.